PRAISE FOR COME HOPE OR HIGH WATER

"A compelling biography. As someone who specializes in treating addiction, I can say firsthand that Candi Cross has successfully told the transformative story of Steve Knuth, whose addiction almost destroyed him. Instead, through recovery and his reemergence as a warrior of hope and action, he resurrects and brings life to rural America and the farms we rely on to feed us."

—*Caprice Haverty, Ph.D., forensic/clinical psychologist*

"Steve Knuth's story is both heartwarming and heartbreaking, yet it is a story that begs to be told. For anyone who has struggled with an addiction, or has known someone who has, this is a must-read. Steve's story is one of hope—hope that through faith, became the reality of a changed life. While the Knuth family has a God-given gift of starting and running successful businesses, Steve's real success is no longer measured alone in what he has attained, but in who he has become—a man of strength, integrity, and wisdom. It is a privilege to call him, 'friend.'"

—*Tom Carlson, former Nebraska State senator*

"Candi Cross provides an unfiltered look at the juxtaposition between the good and bad of an addict. Leading with her own experience of growing up in a single-parent household, Candi showcases the love that endures even with the constant struggle of daily interactions with someone that never recovers. This authentic insight immediately allows the reader to connect with Steve Knuth and his journey of morality, self-reflection, and the impact of someone struggling with alcoholism in a small Midwest community."

—*Kathryn F. Burmeister, Esq.*

"A clear, courageous and insightful true story of the daily struggle of living with alcoholism, addiction and recovery. A genuine and honest look into real-life struggles with mental health, relationships and finding success and a purpose. Steve Knuth, by telling his story, is another voice helping to increase understanding and decrease the stigma of living with addiction and mental health challenges."

—*Lori Maney Lentini, author,* Anxiety Insights: What Gets to Us and What Gets Us Through

"Only through telling our stories and embracing our individual acts of vulnerability will we begin to deconstruct the barrier of stigma and usher in an era when those in need receive the help they deserve. This book is a major step towards accomplishing those goals in a way that both entertains and leaves the reader with a feeling of objective purpose and satisfaction. Bravo!"

—*Jay Shifman, mental health, substance misuse and recovery speaker, host of Choose Your Struggle podcast*

"As evidenced in Candi's striking chronicle of Steve Knuth's life, recognizing your alcoholism is one thing. Committing to lifelong sobriety is quite another, employing every resource you have to fight it and then shape a meaningful life so beneficial for the community. This is the type of story that leaves a mark in the world. There is help. There is hope. There are heroes. Steve's flaws pale in comparison to his own mark."

—*Susan MacKenty Brady, CEO, Simmons University Institute for Inclusive Leadership*

"Sometimes holding on to hope itself is a challenge. I've had the privilege of serving on a drug and alcohol rehab association board with Steve over the past five years. I admire his commitment, passion, and hard work as a leader. He gives tirelessly and often, and his dedication and love for others is obvious. If hope is in short supply for you right now, you need to read his story."

—Dave Hill, president and founder, Mid America Bank

"I couldn't stop reading! Author Candi Cross takes you on a most inspiring, enlightening and transformational journey of one man's unwavering desire to live. His resilience, persistence and determination to transcend his addiction, as well as his passion to improve the lives of farmers, is a true testament that anything is possible. Having lost several close family members to alcoholism, Steve Knuth's story hits home in a big way, as it will for others in these unprecedented and emotionally challenging times, with many struggling to cope with and break free from addiction of any form. Come Hope or High Water is an essential book for this moment and offers great inspiration for anyone ready to heal from this debilitating disease. Massive praise for Candi Cross's book for the many lives it will save."

—Keiya K. Rayne, author, transformational healer, relationship mentor and speaker

"Come Hope or High Water is about life experience, from juvenile bullying to fulfilling highest potential, and everything that can happen in between. This story is not about adversity but about the choices made to handle it in going forward with our lives, resulting in a miracle. Miracles are about restoring to a better state of being. Steve Knuth experienced a miracle that reset his mind from self-destruction to that of self-survival, and he is using his life experience to help others be blessed with miracles."

—*Allen J. Marsh, former CEO, Sapp Bros., Inc.*

"Steve Knuth never had to write this book. Fortunately for all of us he decided to, purposely sharing his story, inspiration and generosity with so many more than those lucky enough to have experienced them already."

—*Taylor Hudson, managing director, Sprague Resources LP*

Escaping Addiction to Save Family Farms
in the Western Corn Belt

COME
HOPE
OR
HIGH
WATER

An Authorized Biography
of Steve Knuth, CEO, AgWest

CANDI S. CROSS

DEDICATION

To James Francis and Susan, for the entryway to this beautiful life.

—Candi

I am far from perfect, but very little today resembles the life I was trying to navigate twenty-two years ago. During the first few years of sobriety, my newly founded business, AgWest Commodities, provided an enormous challenge of which I gave my compete focus. I was both worried about failure and driven to succeed. This intensity and near obsession helped keep me sober, but I was not necessarily a happy person. Early on in sobriety, I didn't know how to be happy or comfortable in this new and sober world. My self-esteem remained bruised and lightening up without being half in the bag was foreign to me. With this thought in mind, I dedicate this book to my amazing wife, Jan, who came into my life in year seven of my sobriety. From our first date, we were extremely comfortable together. She was able to make me laugh; something that had not happened for some time. Her helping me turn that switch back on was the finish touch to becoming a grateful recovering alcoholic.

Jan is an amazing problem solver, which makes her my irreplaceable sounding board. She also has the bigger backbone than most I know, including most men. Jan may only weigh a buck-twenty but when push comes to shove, she will go toe to toe with anyone. She doesn't hide her dislike of bullies and has little tolerance for injustice. Jan is a lot of what I am not and vice versa—and that right there may be the foundation of us being a great team. Whether we are building another flower bed (way too many already) tracking, trapping or saving a dog, building a prop for her haunted house, or watching for an opportunity to help make someone's life better, I can't imagine doing it without her. I love you, Miss Jan!

—*Steve*

CONTENTS

A HERO'S HABITS

It's a Sunday night at the 1930s-inspired Hotel Deco, a stunning gem of a hotel in Omaha, Nebraska. The restaurant has the audacity to offer items like Bison Tartare and 100-Day Wagyu Tomahawk Chop. Too bad I've filled up on typical airplane food! But the lounge is a perfectly suitable place for sipping on wine and creating something, or just staring at the prisms of beautiful textures and colors. My mind is popping with memories though. I'm thinking about my parents, particularly my dad, James Francis Cross.

I don't have many memories of "Fran" without a can of beer in his hand. He taught me how to swim, ride a bike, cook chili, and drive, with a beer in his hand. And until I could drive, he picked me up from school holding a beer under the steering wheel. He listened to my clunky poetry, monologues for acting class, disjointed history presentations, and book reports, all while sipping Stroh's and smoking filter-less Pall Malls.

My dad was not a violent, lazy, or introverted drunk. As a child, he worked in the coalmines of Tennessee to help his parents feed five siblings. As a soldier, he fought in World War II. As a veteran, he drove a truck for Procter & Gamble for decades. As a hero, he jumped in front of a woman whose husband was shooting at her in a bar, and he took a bullet in his heart for a stranger. Surgery to remove it was too dangerous, at least in those days, so the bullet stayed put for the rest of his life. On another night, his friend, a Vietnam veteran who lived in the house behind ours, knelt down in his backyard and shoved a shotgun barrel down his own throat. My dad managed to get the gun away and talked to him clear until sunrise when he tumbled into bed.

I wonder how his life would have been different without alcohol. With him being a single parent during my critical teen years, some conversations were blurry. Some special occasions were missed. Some arguments were nonsensical. Some demands were wildly over the top (like always having the gas tank on full, or never driving in the rain). But we laughed a lot, and despite his alcoholism, he was surprisingly reliable, loyal, affectionate, and decisive.

Alcohol killed him at the age of seventy. Considering that war combat and a bullet in his heart did not take him out, I think he was pretty damned fortunate to live as long as he did.

I'm thinking of him today as I prepare to meet with Steve Knuth, his family and staff in Holdrege, about a three-hour drive "that way." It will be a straight shot through farmland. This part of the country reminds me so much of where I grew up in Batavia, Ohio. Not necessarily all the landscape but the confusing mix of feelings I get. Living in New York City is a different environment and era. If you don't want to confront any recollections of rural life, you simply never have to.

A part of me doesn't want to leave this atmospheric cocoon of Hotel Deco because outside those doors will be quite a story of addiction, with scenes of despair, broken promises to innocent children, a tightly wound cycle of disturbing family patterns, and so many bottles of stolen time sealed away forever.

Yet, it is the type of story I wish I could write about concerning my father. There is recovery. There is success and restitution, salvation, leadership and love, community and industry. Legacy!

Steve has been sober for twenty-one years, and he has had his company, AgWest Commodities, for twenty years. He is purely a beacon of hope for anyone struggling, anyone contemplating whether they want to live or die, anyone desperate to break free from the chains of addiction. I am exceptionally proud to stand behind Steve's story and share it with anyone whose hope may be slipping away.

CHAPTER 1

SOMETHING IN THE SOIL

The air was very busy. Particles of clay, silt, sand, wheat, hay, pine, grain, and honey bees passed through. Conditions changed from cloudy to sunny, from windy to calm, and cold to warm, in a single day.

Nebraska borders the Missouri River, the longest river in North America, and is home to the unique Platte River ecosystem, as well as massive Lake McConaughy, which covers a surface area of 35,700 acres. With all four seasons swooping in and showing their magnificence, there is always something going on in the air.

Spring in the fertilizer and chemical business was always demanding, but when you work in a family operation that was driven by "top shelf" customer service, it was beyond any sane person's definition of *demanding*. It was just like the old saying of "making hay while the sun shines"—the window of opportunity was small during a spring fertilizer season and there was always a gargantuan amount of work to accomplish.

Each and every spring, it was common for employees to clock up to 100 hours per week. There were weeks when the most dedicated folks hit 120 hours on the clock in a seven-day period. Great overtime pay, but that business took a lot out of people and a lot away from families. The family members put in longer hours than the employees, so it was a tough balancing act for an alcoholic to obtain the needed daily fix while maintaining a relatively high level of cognitive ability.

This type of work really stretched the limits of being a functioning alcoholic!

In the twilight world between sleep and waking, Steve Knuth took another sip of Canadian Club whiskey as he tried to prepare a pile of work orders for the next day. At sun-up, approximately thirty people would clock in and their marching orders needed to be well organized to get things efficiently rolling. He leaned back with a grunt. After four nights of frayed naps at his desk, Steve's body, mind, and emotions loudly protested more hours at the fertilizer plant.

And would he even wake up to face another day? He wavered between wanting to and not wanting to. He just craved nothingness. With a fresh, messy divorce, failure as a father, and his liver and lungs in a frying pan from alcohol and cigarettes, Steve didn't have much fight or will left in him. Time caught up again, as he woke to the earliest of the morning folks turning up the lights throughout the office and starting the first of many pots of coffee.

During the gut slot of a spring run, Steve, his other family members, and a few very dedicated employees would run a few of the machines through the night. Then when the normal operators would arrive at about sun-up, this team would resume their office and delegation duties.

If his kids needed to see Steve during a spring run, they would have to go to the plant and discuss in his office or ride with him while he checked fields. There were times when things were so demanding and intense, the kids could not even steal a few minutes of his time. Steve said that you can ask anyone who worked in the family business and they will tell you that words cannot describe the intensity nor the gut determination and dedication that it took to put that much of yourself into a job.

Everything Steve Knuth did, he did full throttle. Love, sex, booze, work, smoking, gambling.

Have you ever stopped to wonder how much the mind can really endure? The physical body? Steve never wanted to do that assessment. As sure as the Nebraska air around him, he just kept thinking—at least about markets and trading—and moving.

For example, when his close friends were in Las Vegas for a family wedding, Steve called them at 7:00 a.m. from Denver International Airport to inform them he was on the way and would be there before lunch. It was a spontaneous decision the night before, but that's just how life was supposed to be lived back then. As a group, they excitedly headed to a blackjack table. They all hung out at the same table for hours; however, Steve lasted for forty hours straight. *Forty hours.* And all the while, drinking and chain-smoking even though they had chosen a non-smoking table. Steve was Mr. Nice Guy and in environments like this, appeared to get away with more than should be possible.

Did you know that in a forty-hour span of time, you can get drunk and somewhat sober back up three different times? One just needs to know when and where coffee becomes the drink of choice for a few hours.

During the 1990s, Steve started betting on college and pro football. He spread out yellow legal pads and handheld calculators (before cell phones). His house was a maze of craziness dotted with yellow everywhere.

Steve eventually bought cases of Canadian Club to make sure there was stock during the busy spring runs or for inclement weather episodes. "We're in the middle of nowhere here!" he asserted. At the same time, Nebraska is America's 9th drunkest state, according to a

2018 analysis from financial news and opinion website, *24/7 Wall St.* It may be in the soil in these parts.

You have to set yourself up for drinking success and you go to great lengths. One day, Steve left a bottle of CC in the front seat of his brand-new Jeep Cherokee. It was a blazing hot day and he never rolled down windows due to dust from truck traffic at the plant. That evening, he opened up the car door to find that the bottle had exploded. The smell knocked him over. He only wished that god-awful smell would stave off the desire to drink again. Unfortunately, it didn't.

Treatment and change would be a long way off from that night when Steve had suicidal thoughts. He desperately wished to see his last reflection in that brown bottle. At the same time, he was at a turning point. His sharp brain gave him so much potential. His hands put in enough effort to fertilize a thousand farms. His ingenuity brought him to the brink of a groundbreaking business. And his generous heart loved many (including a few very special women).

What power would Steve summon to transform? How would he recover from this night? Better yet, how would be recover from this whole era of addiction, guilt, and shame?

AgWest president Paul Mussman describes what Steve would become: "We're in a small, ag-based, rural community. We don't have a ton of highly successful people in our area. Nothing to discount rural America, but rags to riches only happen to a small percentage! They're fewer and far between out here. If there was anyone to represent in rural ag, why should it not be Steve? He has saved farms. He has helped communities. Over forty families in AgWest have benefitted from Steve's vision and discipline. What he has done for our community as a leader, a generous role model, someone who has given back tremendously—it's a big deal. He has helped many people succeed and stay in the area because they are compensated well. These are people here who could go to big cities because they are educated, highly capable people. That's just on one level. Then the spouse may work in the community and be applying their skill set. AgWest provides the anchor that keeps employees and their families here in rural America. What impact is this? It's big. Without AgWest and Steve's vision, how would you recruit people into a place like Holdrege?"

As a state, Nebraska is the largest producer of beef in the States and ranks 3rd in corn production. It's also the largest producer of popcorn in the nation, so pop some and settle in for the story.

CHAPTER 2

WHAT'S GROWING
IN NEBRASKA

Agriculture is the heart and soul of Nebraska.
As the state's leading industry, the impact goes far
beyond the plate, providing Nebraskans with jobs,
significantly contributing to the state's economy, and
touching the lives of its citizens every day. Annually,
production agriculture contributes more than $25 billion
to Nebraska's economy, thanks to the hard work of
Nebraska farmers and ranchers working on 49,100 farms
and ranches spread across more than 45 million acres.
In fact, farms and ranches use 92 percent of Nebraska's
total land area. In sum, a great deal rides on the
industry as both livelihood and food for the nation.

Risk abounds, and there are many faces of a challenge
for farmers on a daily basis. Between weather and
unpredictable commodity prices, every year is a bit
like a crapshoot. Depending on the unknowns, a

farmer's goal ranges from making a healthy return on investment, to holding things together to fight the good fight another year.

In the first decade of the 21st century, the state had a few years that were great beyond folks' wildest dreams. The big driver was the expansion of the ethanol industry and the strong corn demand pushed prices to all-time highs near $8 per bushel. Right on the heels of that record high in the summer of 2008, the financial world collided with the subprime mortgage crisis that ultimately destroyed over 50 percent of the value in the Dow Jones Industrial Average (Dow). When the financial world crumbled into meltdown, everything fell apart. All markets suffered, including agricultural markets. During a six-month period in 2008, corn futures fell from the record high of $7.79 to a late-year low of $3.05 per bushel. It was, by far, the most dramatic boom/bust that agriculture had ever experienced.

Agricultural producers are currently suffering several years of low commodity prices relative to input costs. It is a result of global overproduction. With tariffs from a trade war with China and extremely competitive pricing from other growing regions in the world, U.S. agriculture has been losing market share. Brazil and Argentina, in particular, continue to expand acreage and production. We are truly in a global market and the low-cost producer is going to win. More often than not, the low-cost producer is not the American farmer. Currency valuations also play into the competitive puzzle. When the U.S. dollar is strong compared to the currency of our agriculture competitors, it is a real disadvantage. A weak dollar means foreign buyers can buy more commodities with the same monetary commitment—a good thing for the U.S. farmer!

Supply and demand drive the price of anything and everything. With the global overproduction, U.S. supply has simply outrun demand in recent years. As surplus supplies grow, the commodity price comes under pressure. A lot of marketing firms try to out-guess where they think the markets will trade in the future to help their ag customers market better. The problem with that is that no one can consistently know where markets will trade. It is basically a fool's game and eventually creates serious financial problems for those involved.

In the height of his addiction, Steve was trying to figure out a way to fill this gap and provide market education opportunities for those who wanted to do a better job of selling their production. His passion was serving agriculture and serving family farmers with tools and information to help them stay in business. Unfortunately, weather and natural catastrophes do not wait for heroes.

As I drove through Nebraska to allow this story to unfold, I thought about the unknowns and just how intricate the road to success is. For example, in the spring of 2019, a historic "bomb cyclone" hit much of the middle of the country, bringing heavy rains on top of significant snow cover. The rain, combined with quickly melting snowpack, produced immense amounts of water. To compound the problem, the ground was frozen solid from the long winter, so the water had to run off creating unprecedented flooding across the eastern half of Nebraska.

Weeks after the event, when I was visiting Nebraska for research on this book, communities were still dealing with the consequences and devastation. As rivers tried to handle the tremendous runoff, ice that had covered the waterways broke into huge slabs that banged downstream and eventually clogged together in ice jams, several miles long. "Major and historic" flooding rose along the banks of the Mississippi and Missouri River basins, particularly in Iowa and Nebraska. Three people died.

On March 16, 2019, the Missouri River crested at 47 feet in some areas. The widespread flooding displaced 4,400 people in the region; the entire town of Fremont, Nebraska was surrounded by floodwaters. Although Nebraska bore the brunt of this event and the Missouri Valley remained under water for months, flood warnings were in effect for 9 million people in 14 states.

"This really is the most devastating flooding we've probably ever had in our state's history, from the standpoint of how widespread it is," Nebraska Gov. Pete Ricketts said in the *Omaha Herald*. The warning prompted evacuation orders, schools closing, power loss and water restrictions. Some farms in the region were washed out beyond salvaging. Destroyed! I saw it with my own eyes.

The Washington Post reported $500 million in livestock losses, and $400 million in agricultural losses, due to the flooding.

Then it was 107 degrees in a neighboring town the week I visited Nebraska.

Everyone wanted to talk about the flooding and "the stink" in parts where the soil dried after weeks under stagnant water. There were spots of the interstate with ten feet of water on top of it. I looked at a picture of a van submerged next to a corn stalk. How setting-appropriate.

The reason all this social studies-like and geographical information matters is because the industry needs figures like Steve Knuth, whose eyes were fixed on helping the plight of farmers, even when blurry with intoxication.

One or two farmers commit suicide every day, with dairy farmers being in the highest risk category. One farmer, working sixteen hours a day, has been doing this for forty years, and said he is no further than when he started. A source candidly told me, "Farmers have shot themselves. Farm accidents are pretty easy to pull off, too. Sometimes we don't know that it's suicide. They set it up as an accident because they don't want their families to suffer through unchecked mental illness or hopelessness."

With all these variables, what are the goals on an individual level? What is considered a decent living on farming? Approximately 2,000 acres would be considered an average-size farm in Central Nebraska. A section of ground is *1 mile x 1 mile*, which encompasses 640 acres. At today's prices, it can cost $600 to $700 per acre to raise an irrigated corn crop. So, a 2,000-acre corn operation would invest well over $1 million and then hope that weather, yields, and the price of corn leaves a return on investment at the end of the year. Agricultural debt across the nation is huge and growing.

Commodity markets tend to trade in cycles and when in downturns, this is a tough industry. The past five years have been particularly difficult, and many producers have their backs against the wall. The government has recently stepped in with a $20 billion aid program to help offset the hardships caused by the China trade war and the second wettest spring in U.S. history. Those funds have, no doubt, saved some family farms from demise.

During difficult times like these, suicides increase, and community awareness is elevated in an attempt to be a resource for those fighting a slippery slope. The operation under financial threat may be a generational farm, and no one wants to be the one in a long line of family operators to lose it!

On Main Street in Orleans, it's clear this town of about 300 people is dying. A new house has not been built since the 1980s. Meth cookers move here for the remote location and they rent a house for $250 a month. There's not one person in sight on the drive. However, I learned that the AA meetings in this town were a lifeline for so many people for nearly fifty years.

Steve's friend, Paul P., who attended the Orleans meeting for many years before he passed away, often said: "There's a carton of cigarettes, a bottle of whiskey, and a loaded revolver in the corner of my basement. If I need one of them, I'm going to need them all."

CHAPTER 3

A CLASSROOM OF HIS OWN

Through seventh grade, Steve attended a one-room country schoolhouse (Buffalo School, District 17) located two miles from his family's farmhouse. He often told his kids about the experience of he and his younger brother always walking or riding bikes to school, regardless of the weather, and that it was uphill all the way both to and from school. They never believed him.

He also likes to tell folks he was the smartest kid in his grade school class, leaving out the fact he was the only one in his class through grade 7.

In a one-room school, one teacher taught all eight classes; grades 1 through 8, so the strengths and weaknesses of that teacher were pretty much engrained in kids by the time they moved on to high school. Mrs. Upson taught at Buffalo School for many years and her influence turned out many students with great math skills while lacking some in English and spelling.

The Knuth family lived three miles out of town. Steve's sister, Marilyn, eight years older, recalls: "We had basic needs, but the emotional infrastructure did not exist. How do you know you're not good emotionally if you don't have anything to compare it to? That's the way life was. Farm kids did not get together with other kids. I don't even remember inviting a friend over. I never had a birthday party. None of us kids did. We always had family around, but no friends. We went to a country school and saw 'friends' there only. I did love getting out on the tractor, helping my dad irrigate, and walking the fields. That was the extent of 'hobbies'—and taking care of Steve. As a baby, he gave me purpose."

Marilyn would prove to be integral to Steve's life, making sure he was tended to as a baby, saving him from injury on the farm, and then saving him from taking his life at different points. But she couldn't save him from culture shock or being bullied in the 8th grade, when he joined thirty-four other kids in a bustling classroom. Steve was overweight, which gave the bullies material to openly taunt him with.

Thinking of pummeling those bullies but never getting into one physical fight, he wrestled heavyweight as a sophomore. In senior year, he lost forty pounds and felt much better about himself.

So many years of low self-esteem and naivety had gone unchecked; it was the perfect setup for being an alcoholic. If Steve didn't immediately feel validation, he would sabotage a friendship or intimate relationship. That became part of the death spiral.

The house he grew up in raged with screaming and hollering between Steve's father and grandmother for days on end. For children, this type of environment is very nerve-racking and breeds anxiety in later years. Steve's mother was more of an influence on him. His father treated her badly and left her for another woman late in life. Amazingly, when he had a stroke, his mother took him back in and nursed him until she died first. Many friends and neighbors looked at her as a saint of sorts. After so many years of being treated badly and the embarrassment of losing her husband to another woman, she was his caregiver toward the end of their lives.

Because she internalized so much pain, Steve's mother served as a role model that set him up to be aggressive toward himself. He seldom showed anger toward others.

Even when Steve could barely see straight, he remembers one bartender telling him, "You are the most peaceful drunk I have ever served!"

What most never knew, and even Steve didn't fully understand was that he turned all his anger inward, which was a set-up for depression. This became the foundation of Steve's personality, how so many of his

CHAPTER 4

THE BOTTLE SIGHTING

Steve's family has a deep history in addiction that is alarming. He graduated from high school in 1971 when there wasn't exactly a lot of scientific research or self-help going on.

Unlike many people, Steve didn't start drinking before the last few months of his senior year in high school. Many people in the AA rooms started at an earlier age. But like most people, he started drinking beer—Budweiser, to be exact. This was before the wide selection of light beer we have today, and good ole red-labeled Bud carried a bigger kick than present-day lights.

Around the age of 30, Steve shifted over to CC. For many years, he preferred it because CC and water didn't seem to mess with his allergies, which he had a ton of as a kid, as much as beer. In reality, while this may have been true also, whisky could, naturally, get him to a place he wanted to arrive at quicker than the beer. When he made the switch, it was complete. During the last decade of his addiction, he didn't drink a single beer.

By the way, Steve's drinking career spanned from age 17 to just short of 45 years old.

In his customary low but firm tone, Steve explains: "I'm going to try to share something that I never really understood myself. I have heard similar thoughts from drug users as well. Basically, when one first starts drinking, there is a window of time during the process of getting blitzed that everything seems to be in balance. It is like a feeling of euphoria where everything is good and what is not, can be made to be good. I am capable of making all things good. All is right with the world. Interestingly, the longer one drinks or drugs (the overall career), that window of feeling wonderful about all things diminishes and is even illusive at times. Drug users call it 'chasing the high' but that would also apply to alcohol. It's chasing a feeling that is completely foreign to us in a state of sobriety...a feeling of true serenity. Here's where it would get weird for me and hard to understand. That feeling had a time limit and as I said, the window of time got smaller and smaller. During the course of a span of being drunk, when that feeling drifted away, the consumption would go up. I always assumed it was a subconscious attempt to get the feeling back. Toward the end of my evening drunks, the water in the drink became less and the CC more. At the tail end, I was often drinking straight CC on the rocks and the only water was from melting ice. It was insane in the sense that at that point of a drunk close to or into a blackout stage, the last thing one needed was a more potent drink. But that is exactly how it would unfold for me, night after night. If I was in a bar toward closing time, I would take a half full CC/water back to the bartender and just have them top it off with more CC. So, you can only imagine. When one is close to oblivion, shifting to straight whisky quickly puts you over the edge into the darkness of a blackout.

"Coming off of those nights when out on the town (away from home) was when I would wake up in the morning and delay for hours looking out the window to see if the car was there and if so, was it there without any damage? Would there be blood, or even a person stuck in the grill? I worried about that so much, I couldn't bring myself to look for hours. I am so ashamed of this, but I drove thousands of miles and would not remember. In fact, probably tens of thousands of miles. I SHOULD NOT BE HERE! I SHOULD BE EITHER DEAD OR IN PRISON FOR KILLING SOMEONE ELSE. It hurts to even write that down, but it's certainly true."

Whiskey is more popular than wine in these parts. With its signature advertising, Canadian Club appeals to a large population of men: "What do seven generations of gangsters, smugglers, politicians, ad men, and guys like you have in common? Our best-selling, flagship whisky is where most folks begin their whisky journey. This is the one that started the legend. A giant of Canadian whisky since 1858, it's aged longer than the three years required by law in oak barrels before bottling for the smoothest possible flavor."

Description: Refreshing and smooth. Color: Bright gold. Aroma: Fresh and soft, with an almond nuttiness, hint of peppery spice. (Until you spill a whole bottle in your car!) Taste: Spicy and zesty, complimented with hints of rich oak and sweet vanilla, pleasant sweetness. Finish: Clean, dry, and lingering with subtle oak. Proof: 40% alc./vol. 80 proof.

Steve gravitated to all of its characteristics.

"I've always told people, I was born an alcoholic," he said. "It was just a matter of getting to the alcohol, fixing my eyes on the bottle in the perfect moment."

After those long drives, thankfully, he didn't see blood or glass once! That was a complete miracle. Or was it?

"God takes care of babies and drunks," Steve snickered, but he didn't make this comment in an arrogant way...more with a twinge of nervousness and gratitude.

CHAPTER 5

WELCOME WORKAHOLICS

Steve's older brother, Dewey, was in the highest echelon of overachievers. He was an excellent student in high school and state officer for Future Farmers of America (FFA). He had a sharp mind for business and had a strong start on a farrow-to-finish hog operation (where pigs are bred and raised) before his high school graduation. Dewey started a retail fertilizer and chemical company called TriCo in 1971 and grew it to a 100-employee company when it sold to Cargill in 1997.

In 1976, Steve started working for TriCo. As I mentioned before, the fertilizer industry was extremely high stress during parts of the year, and it seemed to either attract or possibly helped create cigarette smokers and drinkers. TriCo operated with an insane level of customer service. If the customer needed it, the company did anything and everything possible to make it happen. Every year, up against the weather, family members and the most dedicated of employees would work a few forty-hour stints. And if rain didn't materialize to shut things down by the end of one of the marathon runs, those folks would go home for a shower and a few hours of sleep before returning to the grind. (See, by the time Steve got to that blackjack table, he could withstand forty hours of gambling, drinking, and smoking!)

Steve managed one of three loading facilities and out of his plant the crew would run six or seven commercial spray rigs with twenty-five trucks hauling fertilizer to those machines across four different counties.

It was not unheard of for employees to log 100-hour weeks during the two-month spring run. With the stress level over the top, Steve would drink coffee all day long and then alcohol all evening until his day would finally end. He would be so immersed in work at times that he would have three cigarettes burning simultaneously. The secondary smoke in his office could be cut with a knife. That seems odd today but understand that Steve remembers when you could smoke on airplanes, and he smoked while he was in the hospital for a few days in the early 70s. The world has changed so much in a few decades!

Amazingly, Steve always had his head in learning everything he could about agriculture, its chemistry, and seed selection. Simultaneously, he observed that farmers were great at producing a crop, but spent little time learning the skills and tools necessary for successful marketing of their production. Like any business, a farm needs to turn a profit for long-term viability and selling at good vs. poor prices can make the difference.

One day, TriCo held a sales meeting and in between yawns, someone was supposed to come up with a catchphrase for marketing. Avis Car Rental had coined the phrase "We try harder" back in the 1960s. Given the high level of customer service at TriCo, someone brought up that well-known slogan and another employee quickly came back with, "No, we try longer!" That got a laugh from the group because it was dead-on correct in every sense.

In his twenties, Steve and his two brothers started a trucking company to move alfalfa hay, and they scored a contract with the local cheese factory to ship their product to Salt Lake City. Steve managed this company and also drove half of the time. Whenever he would get through Norton, Kanas and drive past Valley Hope, an alcohol treatment center that had started in 1967, it would give him pause. In those early years of the world addressing alcoholism, the whole thing seemed a bit mysterious or even taboo. Folks just didn't talk about or understand the disease of alcoholism. If someone would disappear for thirty days, the story was that they "went off to get the cure." How naïve everyone was back then—there is no cure for alcoholism or drug addiction.

Finding a way to live in abstinence is the answer, but that is certainly not a cure.

As they say in AA meetings, "Once pickled, you can never again be a cucumber."

Steve knew at an early age he was in the throes of addiction and whenever traveling past the Valley Hope facility, he would think to himself, *someday I will have to find out what that place is all about.*

It took twenty-something years to walk through the Valley Hope doors the first time.

In the meantime, everyone around him was getting married. Yes, "women have a biological clock," but he surely had a clock ticking, too! All of his friends were leaving the house party or small-town bar while Steve was still partying. It felt like he was doing something wrong—particularly since in his twenties, he had finally found a tribe. He didn't desire to be the loner in the bar, just like he never got used to being the loner in the schoolhouse.

Brenda, an attractive woman, came into town from the West Coast to visit her sister, who worked for TriCo. She introduced her to Steve. In no time, they went on a couple of dates, and on the second, he met her three-year-old and five-year-old daughters. While waiting on Brenda to finish getting ready, the youngest one, Dawn, jumped on his lap and asked if she could call him "Daddy."

He recalls, "I was screwed at that moment! It was similar to that famous line in the Jerry McGuire movie, 'You had me at hello'. Well, he was had when that little three-year-old girl asked that one heavy question. Dawn was the catalyst for Steve asking their mother to marry him. He adopted the girls. His brand-new daughters were Ronda and Dawn. They needed a father, but their mother did not need a raging alcoholic. No sooner than everyone settled in as a family, trouble erupted.

You can't mix and match marriage with alcoholism and expect silver- and gold-plated anniversaries. As newlyweds and parents, Steve and Brenda didn't get along; in fact, their relationship seemed to leek poison into the whole community. The air around them was just not good.

Still, their son, Jamie, was born in 1977. Steve was twenty-four years old and his "toolbox was already empty."

Between his wife's "berating sessions," which may have been a direct result of her bitterness toward Steve's constant absence and escalating addiction, and his inadequacies stirring, life was becoming a blur for Steve. He had managed to woo clients to the plant, however, who became long-life friends. On far too many nights, they partied as Brenda cared for the kids. Their rollercoaster of a marriage lasted for nearly twelve years before she filed for divorce. For Brenda, she had escaped a bad relationship with another man in California and aimed to start over with her daughters in Nebraska. Steve had first resembled a knight in shining armor, not a knight soaked in alcohol. Separation was inevitable and probably should have happened sooner.

Sensing a low point, Steve's friend, Jeff Swanson, had a long conversation with him on the phone. By this time, Steve had built a house right across the county road from the fertilizer plant. Jeff knocked on the door soon after putting down the phone. He wanted to confiscate Steve's guns.

It turns out that Jeff did not remove the guns; however, he stayed with Steve until the sunrays could be seen through the curtains.

We probably all know this, but it's worth stating that alcohol and relationships don't mesh well. If you drink long enough, you destroy everything around you. You're out of options and this is where suicidal thoughts come in. People don't see an option. The pain is so deep they can't take it anymore. The farm country at the center of this story contains people right now who think the world will be better without them. There is nothing "selfish" churning in their minds, in contrast to what some of the outside world says. They just have so much pain within.

CHAPTER 6

SHAKY HAND ON THE IGNITION

One of the most important relationships in Steve's life took shape when he was at the depths of low self-esteem. He was coming off the marriage to Brenda and was beat to a pulp. Jo had just finalized a divorce of her own and because they were both in great need of feeling better, their compatibility and chemistry ignited an amazing, almost overwhelming, front end of a relationship.

In hindsight, it was immediately a very co-dependent relationship. That said, Jo did so much for Steve's self-image. She was beautiful, outgoing, and adored by all who knew her. Jo gracefully stepped between friends who were common middleclass folks, and a crowd of the so-called "important" people. She was a phenomenal woman and Steve truly felt as though God put her in his path at just the right time.

Meantime, in 1988, the Corn Belt suffered a major drought. The corn market shot up to an all-time high. At Steve's fertilizer plant, they had a prehistoric market quote machine that delivered ten-minute delayed prices from the Chicago Board of Trade. As the drought began, the corn market began going up the daily limit. Note: Most commodities futures have daily price limits and once reached, trading ceases for the day. During the 1988 drought, the price of new crop December corn ran from $2.35 per bushel to nearly $3.70 in just three weeks. During that time, there were multiple days where trading stopped due to hitting the daily trading price limit.

Steve had never paid a great deal of attention to agricultural markets prior to the drought, but he became mesmerized by the action and could not help but wonder who was making all this money.

Soon, his brain lit up with interest in the markets. He didn't have enough money to trade, but he voraciously read books about it.

He amassed a library of commodity books and attended some high-dollar conferences with the most well-known commodity gurus. One he attended in Chicago cost $2,000 to get in the door for a weekend event. That was back when $2,000 was a serious chunk of change for a fertilizer plant manager in South Central Nebraska.

Steve went on a tangent of trading for a few years, trying to figure out how to beat the markets. Being an alcoholic, nothing ever had a good ending, unfortunately. He was in the throes of active addiction. He remembered telling his counselor in his second trip through the Valley Hope treatment center that he wasn't sure if he was trading at his drinking or drinking at his trading. In hindsight, it was both.

Steve created the beginning of his romantic undoing in the fall of 1989 when he asked Jo to marry him. Feeling rather inept on the jewelry front, he asked a friend of Jo's to help him select a ring. He proudly and a little clumsily presented her a perfectly polished diamond ring on the porch of her house one evening at the same time a historic shoot-out was taking place in Holdrege. A couple of escaped convicts from a Colorado prison ran into the law in Holdrege and shots were exchanged during a chase around town.

It didn't come close to Jo's house, so other than a chorus of police sirens, they didn't realize what was happening. The evening of their engagement will forever be marked in the history books by the shootout in Holdrege though!

The reason this was the beginning of their problems is that Jo wanted to wait to let folks know until the next week when her "pitch-bitch" club met. That's what they called themselves. They typically did more drinking and socializing than playing cards, and smelling a party,

Steve met up with the whole crew later that evening at the most popular bar in Holdrege. They closed the place down in a rambunctiously good time.

Out of the blue, around 2:00 in the morning, Steve woke Jo and told her he needed help...for alcoholism. He wanted to check into Valley Hope. She called someone they knew, Mike C. who had been through treatment the previous year. Before the sun came up, Steve was checking into Valley Hope in Norton, Kansas, the very place that he had driven past so many years before and somehow knew he would be there someday.

A sad sidebar to that night: Mike C. was happy to get out of bed in the middle of the night to help a struggling alcoholic. Mike had been sober for less than a year. Approximately a year after this night and a couple years after Mike C. sobered up, he took his own life. Mike C. was in his mid-thirties and he left behind a wife and two young daughters. There is a saying in AA (AA is full of sayings, by the way) that "we could no longer imagine life with or without alcohol." That must have been where Mike C. found himself that night.

It's no surprise that Steve had no idea what Valley Hope, or any rehab for that matter, was all about before checking himself in that night.

On the first morning, Steve was there in a daze and hung over when a few patients were ready to leave, and they had their "cup-hanging" ceremony. This is the first exercise of the day when folks are ready to exit rehab.

Steve walked into the daily activities.

His first shock was something called the "hug line." Mind you, Steve Knuth was a red-blooded, mid-thirties-year-old male, so scoring the chance to hug the female patients on a daily basis wasn't bad, but the hug line included everyone. He was a pretty conservative guy who didn't grow up in a house with a lot of physical affection. With that, an alarm went off.

Alert! Alert! Too many unknowns in this place.

Though he had noble intentions, maybe checking in had been another one of those bad, drunken decisions. Even so, Steve hugged all the guys in the joint and didn't really have a choice.

The next shock was watching some folks hang their cups. Looking around the room at the hundreds of cups on the wall, it became obvious that painting and "decorating up" a cup was not going to be optional. Steve didn't consider himself to be artsy. He would put off the cup until near the end of the month.

With a huge grin, he recalls: "I ended up painting it up with a few meaningful things I could talk about."

The idea behind the cup hanging is that at the end of a full year of sobriety, you can come back and pick up your cup and briefly talk to the current group about your years' experience.

With the cup hanging in the balance, Steve only stayed sober for a few weeks, so there was no picking up the cup in his future. He hadn't wanted to go through the ritual in the first place, but it also symbolized a failure.

Jo had seemed supportive and even spent a few days at Valley Hope for "family week." But shortly after Steve returned home, she informed him how hurt she was that he chose the night of their engagement announcement to head off to treatment. It was awful timing and Steve would always regret how that unfolded. In truth, he suspected that in his subconscious, he was excited about the engagement to this lovely, vivacious woman, but he knew that a marriage would not last if he were drinking. Looking back, he admits to panicking (while drunk that night) and unfortunately, decided that was the moment to try to get better. That decision, more than likely, set in motion the beginning of the end to the relationship.

From that event, resentment grew over time and in the fall of 1992, Steve eventually sabotaged the relationship with a drunken one-night stand.

CHAPTER 7

HUG LINE

Steve had logged thousands of miles on the road that he should have never driven, but astoundingly, he was never in trouble with the law. Still, his world squashed into other types of jail cells.

In 1992, that senseless affair threw him over the edge. In those vulnerable minutes of not feeling validated by Jo, who he adored, he had acted out. It was an emotionally fatal mistake and Steve was closer to suicide than ever. He drove around on country roads north of Holdrege one evening shortly after they split and was looking for the right bridge and the appropriate courage that would take care of the pain.

He was without options—and there aren't many bridges with a steep drop-off in this part of the state.

Within two weeks of the breakup, Steve summoned enough sense to return to Valley Hope. What's different about treatment and rehabilitation now is insurance.

The average treatment stay at Valley Hope is sixteen days due to insurance. Are two weeks ever enough to heal any disease? Absolutely not. Put another way, are two weeks enough to eradicate a basic habit? It takes at least three weeks, according to psychologists and neurologists. The longer you keep people engaged in change, the better.

Enter the cup ceremony again. Valley Hope throws away the unclaimed cups about every two years to make room for more. When Steve returned to Valley Hope just over three years from the first rehab, during the first counseling session he had with Carol, his same counselor from the first rehab, she opened up the cupboard behind her desk and pulled out his cup. She had saved it from the typical demise, thinking she would see Steve again!

Steve thought it was cool that she retrieved it from the storage room for him to use that cup for a second hanging. He needed something added for semblance because he was in a much darker place than the first rehab. Steve decided to put it in a plastic bag and drop it in the parking lot. He then glued all the pieces back together and added a few comments illustrating his brokenness at that point in time. That made the cup effort pretty simple and actually quite meaningful for him.

He also wrote a "farewell letter" to alcohol that he read at the cup hanging, but the weirdest thing happened to him while reading to the patient group. Steve Knuth had worked hard all his life to not show much emotion, and he rarely cried. He had never cried in public and here in this world of broken, regretful people crying freely, he had gone through two complete rehabs and never shed a tear that anyone saw. Still, at this ceremony, Steve started breaking up while saying goodbye to alcohol. The deeper he got into the letter, the worse it was. He barely made it through the letter without sobbing.

Alcohol, my dearest friend,

For 21 years, we have run together. A long friendship by any standard. We were best of friends because when everyone else failed us, we were always there for each other. All the hours we shared. All the crazy times we had together. We were like kids riding on the edge, knowing we were indestructible and always in the right. Twenty-one years of friendship through the good times and the bad.

Well, my friend, all things must come to an end. I know there will be times that I miss you, but life must go on. I can no longer run at the pace you dictate. I should we getting older and wiser, but in your company, I seem to be more immature than ever. You have taken me places and we have done things that make me hang my head in shame. It seems there is no limit lately to how much time we spend together and what we are capable of doing. I cannot continue to run with you on this insane course or I will surely die. Only by the grace of God have I made it this far with you.

I am sure you won't miss me, you have such a knack for finding friends. Friends that have yet to see the crazy times you offer.

Believe me, I will never forget you, but I pray to God I will never again call upon you for your company.

Your past friend,

Steve K

Reading the words of a goodbye to something Steve had been dependent on for so many years, these minutes of all minutes, brought so much emotion to the surface. This only seemed to substantiate his "nice guy syndrome." In this treatment round, he had to wear a sign that said, "Nice guys don't always finish last." With nonstop regret and yearning crisscrossing his heart, Steve wanted Jo back. She couldn't get over the affair though. Once Jo got past a fortieth birthday party she threw for him, she began dating someone else. Despite the cup, despite the tears and letter, despite the bone-grinding resilience, Steve picked up the bottle after eight painstaking months of sobriety. As if the series of events were yesterday, Steve's face drooped when he said, "I very much regret all the people I hurt during my twenty-seven years of drinking, but what I did to Jo sits right up at the top of that list. A special lady that helped me through a terrible time!"

CHAPTER 8

IT'S LONELY AT THE TOP

The last meal of the day, or "supper", would always come for Steve right between the last drink of the night and bed. There is an old saying that "you don't want to screw up a $50 drunk with a $10 meal," and for a true alcoholic, that is absolutely the truth. You drink until you're done and then worry about sustenance.

Late one Friday night, while Steve was finding something to eat, he opened up his back-patio door to relieve himself. It was a door that was right off of his kitchen. The ability to take a leak most anywhere is one of the perks of living in rural America. The closest family lived half mile down the road. His house had two perfectly good bathrooms but just four steps from the oven and you could take aim at the whole world. It was something he had done hundreds of times but that night, he was particularly sloshed. He lost his balance in the middle of the task and ended up taking a swan dive off of the three-foot patio. Steve will admit he wished he had a video, as he was sure he could have received style points.

His landing was slightly buffered as he smashed a white chair made of PVC to smithereens. The impact temporarily knocked him silly, but he soon gathered his bearings. He was lucky he did come to, as the temperature that night was in the forties and he was sprawled out in the yard in only his briefs. Exposure would have done Steve in had he been down for the count. As drunk as he was, he realized by the excruciating pain in his chest that something bad had happened. He never made it fully to his feet. He crawled back into the house and eventually to his bed on his hands and knees.

As any good alcoholic would do, he ignored the pain the best he could as he drank his way through the weekend.

Early Monday morning, the alcohol wore off and Steve couldn't take the pain any longer. As if calling up a friend on the way to meet her for supper, he called the hospital at about 5:00 a.m. and told them he was coming! It turns out that Steve had two broken ribs. When they offered to send an ambulance, Steve told them he was just going to drive himself and someone needed to meet him in the parking lot because the idea of getting out of the vehicle on his own did not seem possible. He conducted every physical step in a fog.

Steve's current wife, Jan, always enjoys referencing his bucking porch when that story is told.

Drinking is strapped with risk!

Entrepreneurs are risk takers. Steve has lived his life on the edge, so it's ingrained in him. In ways, so are isolation and loneliness.

Alcoholics reach a point where people intrude on the parade of their addiction. The alcohol gets in between relationships but addicts subconsciously yet somehow deliberately push people away because they can't drink what they want to drink. Once they conquer this destination, shoving everyone out of their way, it's a profoundly lonely place to be.

Steve's kids always ended up with their mom at Christmas. He had nobody. He spent several Christmases alone. On one Christmas eve, out in the country, these feelings of overwhelming loneliness hit Steve with force. He decided that he couldn't stand it any longer and he couldn't get cleaned up and headed toward a bar fast enough. Steve could barely get showered and dressed without stumbling, but he managed to look like a groomed human being. Steve hopped into his truck and drove to a neighboring small town. (There are a lot of small towns to choose from in the state of Nebraska!) Steve pulled onto Main Street and all three bars were closed. Shocked and crestfallen, Steve checked twice.

The ten-mile drive back home that night was the saddest and loneliest moments of his life. He realized that everyone, even the drunks, had someplace to be on Christmas eve.

CHAPTER 9

DOGS ARE DRINKING BUDDIES TOO

Snoopy, the dog, was Steve's best friend during the darkest of times.

He arrived in the summer of 1994 and not necessarily to a warm welcome. Steve had been back in the drinking saddle for a couple of years. Steve's son, Jamie, had moved in with him at age fifteen and he was now ready to start his senior year of high school.

Jamie and one of his sisters went to Kearney, about forty minutes away, to do some shopping, as they were leaving for California to visit relatives in a few days. To Steve's dismay, Jamie came home with a pup from a shelter in Kearney. He said "he" wanted a dog, but Steve had a hunch that his son felt he needed company in the form of a furry friend.

Snoopy was a cute, energetic, little guy that was obviously going to grow into a big one. Jamie had already named him "Snoopy" by the time they arrived. Steve wasn't pleased, but he couldn't bring himself to make Jamie take him back either.

Within a few days, Jamie left for a three-week trip to California. During that time, Snoopy bonded with Steve in what turned out to be a life-long bond. He became Steve's dog, his shadow. He grew into a 100-pound, long-legged beauty. The Knuths all guessed he was a combination of golden retriever with long legs that indicated some greyhound mixed in. Whatever breed he was, Snoopy gave Steve unique meaning when he desperately needed it.

Alcohol damages some of your 86 billion brain cells, or neurons, which send electrical and chemical messages within the brain and between it and other parts of the body.

Still, Steve retained what he learned about the markets and that knowledge laid the foundation of him trying as hard as anyone he knew to beat the markets and educate producers. He racked up a lot of sleepless nights during his quest to become a full-time trader.

In 1990, Steve passed the "Series III" test to become a commodity broker. He hoped to assist a few of his fertilizer customers with improving the marketing of their production, but he mainly wanted to justify through a few commissions the $500 per-month quote machine he had at his desk. It allowed him instant access to the Chicago Board of Trade and the Chicago Mercantile Exchange markets, something he needed for the trading he was trying to perfect.

He operated the part-time brokerage with approximately twenty customer clients from 1990 to 1997 when his brother sold the fertilizer operation to Cargill. He had to argue at several levels of Cargill corporate to maintain his part-time brokerage, but they eventually succumbed and deemed his small brokerage as a pilot program. Cargill had strict rules about employees trading so without a special exemption, the dream of trading and operating a brokerage may have ended then and there.

Steve hung around for eighteen months after the sale to Cargill. Overnight, the family operation of more than 100 employees merged with an industry giant of tens of thousands of employees in various countries. It was quite a culture shock. Steve ran one of the loading facilities.

Day one, after the sale was completed, Cargill brought a dozen or more folks from Minneapolis corporate to get things organized and to instill the Cargill way. Within a day or two, someone presented Steve with a 1,000-page "operations manual." He really did not know what that meant! As a small family organization, employees simply got up each day and did whatever needed done to make things work. They had not played by roles or rules of engagement. They didn't have policies or titles. A book of policies, procedures and rules seemed beyond comprehension.

Ultimately, Steve was fortunate enough to leave with enough money to make it a year without a salary and that allowed him a shot at taking the part-time commodity brokerage full-time.

Steve and Snoopy started their own business as a one-man, one-dog shop. Steve hoped that he could make enough money to bring along Susan, his bookkeeper from the fertilizer plant. They were also dating at the time. He worked nonstop to get enough customers for the two of them. In just six months, Susan made the leap and joined Steve and Snoop in the exciting new venture called AgWest Commodities.

Steve's immediate success could be attributed to his unique knowledge and loyal customer base since the 1980s. They clung to their trust in him. Some of them knew about his alcoholism, but they almost separated it from his business identity.

Roger Johnson and his wife, Rhonda, operate a farm of 4,000 acres and have two fulltime employees. During harvest, production takes about thirteen employees. They try to get every bushel out of every acre to make a profit. (The flooding and wet spring of 2019 is reducing some of the U.S. corn and soybean production.) Usually it takes a drought to get the price up. Out of college, Roger did crop consulting for five years. His parents owned land but didn't farm. Roger started one with a tractor and one little piece of equipment. First-generation farmers are rare in the state of Nebraska. His wife thought he would be a banker!

When Roger priced all his own grain and hoped to sell it during good times, his stomach turned, and he was often upset. However, when he partnered with Steve in his basement business, he gained total peace of mind by being covered for downside price movement via the tools of the brokerage trade. Today, when he hears dire updates on the markets, it doesn't matter as much because of his partnership with AgWest.

Roger explains the basis for one of his products, ethanol, which is largely used for fuel and food and has had a profound impact on America's farming landscape, with dozens of giant distilleries stacked up in the country's Corn Belt.

"Ethanol got a bad reputation when it first came out, but the mainstream media had it wrong. They were pitching it as food being used for fuel. People don't need the field corn that they drive by. The corn is used for cattle feed after the alcohol is extracted so there is little food value lost in the distilling process."

It is not unusual that folks on the coasts or more metropolitan areas ("city folks") do not understand rural America and how the American farmer produces what they find on their grocery store shelves and in the meat cases. There is an old saying that goes: "In your lifetime, you will occasionally need a doctor, a pharmacist and a minister but you need a farmer three times a day!" With approximately twenty-five operating ethanol plants utilizing the state's abundance of corn as the main feedstock, Nebraska produces more than 2 billion gallons of renewable fuel annually. Meanwhile, distillers' grains, a co-product of ethanol production, is important as both a domestic livestock feed ingredient and as a foreign export product. The linkage between corn, ethanol and livestock production has become known as Nebraska's "Golden Triangle," and Roger attributes Steve's decades-long partnership for playing a part in it.

CHAPTER 10

LAST REHAB ON THE LEFT

With the pain over the loss of Jo at more of a distance, Steve saw an opportunity for romance and ultimately, marriage, with Susan, a bright and ambitious star in the community. Romance is not an elixir for addiction, however.

Steve had spent the previous two years accepting the fact that he was an alcoholic and that it was going to kill him. What few prayers Steve said in those previous two years was just before he would fall asleep or pass out as it was, were prayers to just let it be over. "I do not want to wake up in the morning" had become his mantra.

The reality is that the in-between stage of striving to become sober and believing you will come out the other side, without tangible evidence, is a limbo without an internal explosion to flip the switch. Unfortunately, all the love in the natural world or a vision of the future is not enough. Addiction's strongest competitor is a higher power.

Steve had no intentions to go into a third treatment center. It was embarrassing to come in and out. He had come to the grips that he was an alcoholic and therefore, his body and mind required alcohol. *I'll die this way*, he told himself over and over again.

Again, Steve had trouble with blackouts that started early on, which is an indication that someone has a problem with their indulgence. He could easily drink to black-out stage. You literally walk, drive, try to talk, but you don't have a conscious clue as to what is going on.

One Sunday evening in February of 1998, Steve went to a bar in Oxford, where he grew up and twelve miles from his house across gravel roads. Many of the bars in Nebraska offer Keno, a lottery-like gambling game, and Steve decided to pass the time by playing something the locals had tagged "chicken Keno."

In Keno, the strategy is that players make a wager and choose some numbers ranging from 1 through 80. Players can choose between 1 and 20 numbers with each amount of numbers having a set payout based on how many of the player's numbers actually come up. Keno in Nebraska is a statewide electronic system with numbers chosen by a random generator. The maximum payout for Keno in Nebraska was $25,000 back in the

1990s. This point is important concerning the game of chicken Keno.

There is an interesting side note about gambling in Nebraska. Keno is the only form of gambling the state allows. Las Vegas-type casinos have been built across the U.S. in the past twenty years, but multiple attempts by operators to change laws allowing them to build in the state have been rebuffed by the Nebraska Unicameral, the supreme legislative body of the state of Nebraska.

In chicken Keno, the strategy is to pick one number and place a bet. As long as that number does not come up, you double the last bet for the next game. Understand that twenty numbers are chosen out of eighty possible numbers each time a Keno game runs. Therefore, the odds of your number coming up are 1 in 4. The payout for hitting a single number is 3 to 1 so if you place a $2 bet, the winning payout is $6. If your number does not come in on the first game, the next bet is $4, and the winning payout would be $12. If your number doesn't come in on the second game, the next bet would be $8, and the winning payout would be $24. And this sequence continues until the number eventually comes in.

As Steve explains, the net earnings when a number finally hits is equal to the last bet plus the first bet. Here is an example of the math. In this example, the chosen number comes in on the 8th game so the following bets had been placed: $2 - $4 - $8 - $16 - $32 - $64 - $128 and a $256 bet on the 8th Keno game when the chosen number finally hits. The payout is three times the last bet or $768 in this case: ($256 X 3). That is the winning proceeds, but through the 8 games, $510 had been bet or invested. So, the net winnings in this example came to $768 - $510 = $258, which is the equivalent of the last bet of $256 + the first bet of $2.

In theory, if one just keeps doubling the bet the number will eventually come in and it is a slam dunk to profitability! Not so fast though.

As with all gaming, there are rules that mess with the most logical of strategies. In the case of Keno, the maximum payout of $25,000 put a lid on the theory of chicken Keno working as long as one continued to double the bet. In simple terms, once a Keno bet went above one-third of the maximum $25,000 payout, the chicken Keno strategy was: blown up. So, beginning with a $2 bet, how many games without the chosen number coming up could be played before the strategy failed? A person's chosen number needs to show up within 13 games or it is GAME OVER! On the 13th game, the last bet is $8,192, which would have a payout of $24,576 or just under the maximum $25,000. If the chosen number did not come in by the 13th game, the 14th game wager would be $16,384 and with a maximum $25,000 payout, the theory no longer works.

That is a long explanation to the logic of a dangerous gambling strategy, but that was the type of thing that got Steve's blood pumping. Always running the math on various strategies...always a risk taker... always chasing the thrill.

That particular Sunday night, he decided to pass time in the small town bar drinking and playing chicken Keno. He played a total of 12 games without his number coming in and by then, he was into a complete blackout drunk. The excitement and tension of needing his number to show up required an escalated consumption of CC and waters. What started out as an innocent evening out in one of the bars in his hometown turned into an $8,000 Keno loss and he was a drunken mess. How true this story rings for all alcoholics—turning a simple, boring evening into something awful, sometimes life altering. This event became life altering for Steve.

Steve got so drunk the gal running the bar that evening drove him home. At this stage of his life, he didn't have that kind of money to lose! Steve was in a blackout completely and he said something that scared her for his wellbeing. She got him home safely around 11:00 that evening and then called one of Steve's relatives out of concern.

Steve came out of the blackout at about 2:00 a.m. He was sitting at his kitchen table in his home, talking to people. This is the first conscious thing he knew for several hours and to this day, he remembers looking around the room and saying, "What the fuck are all you people doing here in my house?"

Susan was sitting there tearfully with a couple of family members and an employee with TriCo who had recently been through a treatment program. So, this guy who was never going back for another rehab round, this guy who had accepted his alcoholism as his plight in life, this guy who just wanted to drink himself to death and get it over with, had said something in a complete blackout that set the wheels in motion for yet another try. The folks in his house that night had devised the game plan before he came out of the blackout, and he wasn't getting out of this deal. Looking back, he firmly believes that God had a hand in how things unfolded that night. It certainly was not by his desire or doing to head off to another rehab.

Steve went to a treatment center in Minnesota, but not before begging his banker to loan him the money to cover the check he wrote to cover the Keno game the night before! Teary-eyed and near breaking down completely, Steve talked with his banker and close friend, Don Ehrke, about what had happened and why he needed the money. Banking rules were not as strict twenty years ago, so Don's willingness to cover the debacle likely had more to do with compassion than good business sense.

His bag was already packed when he arrived at the bank. From there, Susan and a friend, who had recently sobered up, headed north for Minnesota. After a ten-hour drive and plenty of time to think, Steve was beat to a pulp when they pulled up to this treatment center.

It was a cool setting on the bank of one of the 10,000 lakes in Minnesota. The facility was built around what was once Hubert Humphrey's lake house. Humphrey was a U.S. senator from Minnesota and Lyndon Johnson's vice president from 1965 to 1969.

Steve hated this rehab for more than one reason. It wasn't Valley Hope. It didn't have that welcoming, loving feeling associated with the Valley Hope program. Beyond that, sitting next to a frozen lake in February, he came down with one of the worst colds ever while there. Being a good alcoholic, he blamed it on the fact that smokers, which were the majority there, had to stand outside in the wintery cold to get their fixes. Another weird thing about that part of the world was the size of their mosquitoes. The weather warmed up for a few days toward the end of his stay and Minnesota mosquitoes started showing up. They were nothing like a Nebraska mosquito; they were more like a small bird. "Creepy, dammed things."

One night about halfway through his twenty-six days at this facility, Steve knelt down on his hands and knees beside his bed and literally gave up. There was no fight left. He had no answers. That is *surrender.* That point of surrender is so critical to turning the corner with an addiction. Steve had fought it for ten years. He even tried without the help of treatment centers multiple times, thinking he could work himself through this. After all, Steve was a smart man.

However, everyone has a different bottom.

At this treatment center, one of the patients, a woman, had stabbed her husband to death and she was there trying to sober up. That is a pretty tough bottom! Steve had spent ten years separating himself from "these people." He didn't want to be one of them, didn't want to be a loser. They had all kinds of problems covering a checkerboard of wrecked lives.

Coming out of the first treatment center, Steve was more convinced than ever that he didn't have a problem. "These people" had been in and out of jail and looked twenty, thirty years older than their actual ages. During his second trip through, Steve's counselor said, "If you spent half your time trying to find a commonality between you and 'these people', you might get something out of this! You keep trying to set yourself apart from everybody." This was the first time Steve was told that if he didn't change, he was going to die from something called terminal uniqueness.

Steve was at his whit's end and simply ready to give up. He was either going to give up on life itself or give up on his ability to fight the good fight on his own. Thankfully, he chose the latter and amazingly, the idea and process of staying sober became much easier than had been the case before.

He asserts, "Don't get me wrong, it wasn't a cake walk but that moment of surrender, or acceptance, was a milestone on my path to true recovery."

With Steve coming out of his third rehab, he could no longer resist the support of a sponsor, so Keith Poyser basically adopted him as his teenage-like forty-five-year-old man. Keith had watched him go in and out of the program over a ten-year span of time and firmly decided to sponsor Steve, whether he wanted one or not. At that time, Keith had been sober over twenty years and had served as a sponsor and mentor for many newcomers to the program of Alcoholics Anonymous.

According to Keith's wife of sixty-five years, Dolorous, he sponsored quite a few people throughout his forty-plus years of sobriety before his death in 2017. He religiously went to three meetings a week, always showing up early to make sure the room temperature was acceptable and most importantly, that the coffee was on. AA folks love their coffee! Throughout the years, Dolorous started and was the mainstay person for the local Al-Anon group that met each Wednesday evening. As a couple, they were extremely dedicated to helping people escape addiction.

"I can't even get a beer down!" Dolorous laughs. "Keith would 'clean up' a table and drink the remainder of everyone else's drinks. When we visited my oldest girl in college, I couldn't figure out how he got drunk before. He had liquor tucked in his boot. As a source of pride and sobriety, he kept a can of beer in the refrigerator throughout the forty years of his sobriety! It never exploded." (I saw the unopened can.)

Keith started calling Steve on a fairly regular basis. In turn, Steve started leaning on him when things were bothering him, or he was having a particularly difficult day. He had many of those early on. Without Keith's persistence and regular check-ins when Steve missed a meeting or two, he insists that he would not have gotten strong enough to maintain—when long-term sobriety set in.

Keith often called Steve when he would miss a meeting or for sure, after missing two meetings. One of his favorite lead-in lines during these calls was, "Word on the street is that you are living there with an idiot and you need to occasionally get out of there." The reason that was poignant is the fact that Steve lived alone. The most dangerous place for an alcoholic is in his own mind.

There were some other key players in Steve finally finding sobriety, but Keith was an absolute godsend in the process. Steve will forever be grateful for Keith's persistence and believing that he was worth the time.

CHAPTER 11

PASSIONATE SADNESS

Drunks are manipulators. Steve left his last treatment center in early March, and on June 24, 1998, he decided that Susan wasn't treating him quite right. She wasn't giving him appropriate kudos for four months of sobriety and in his typical fashion clamoring for validation, he went into an "I'll show you" mode.

This is a typical feature of the alcoholic mindset.

Steve drove to a town thirty miles away where no one would likely know him and bought the biggest bottle of CC ever manufactured. He then returned home to partake alone.

Steve hadn't drunk in months and dipped deep into the bottle that night. Consequently, he was so hung over that he couldn't go into work the next morning. Susan had a good idea what happened when he called in sick, and Steve assumed that sometime during the day, she would call or come to his house to apologize for "pushing him over the edge."

She did come later that morning and to his surprise, she obliterated his self-pity and arrogance. It was a short conversation with a very clear message. "If this is what you want to do, we are done for good...it is over." Steve was stunned by her reaction and attitude.

That was one of the longest afternoons Steve ever had. Thinking. *Debating.* Thinking. *Debating.* Would he succumb to death by alcohol or try to regroup and start with the first twenty-four hours of sobriety once again? By late afternoon, Steve had decided to regroup and tried to call Keith. He was nowhere to be found and Steve was at a critical juncture. Needing support, he found a number for another old-timer, Wayne A., who regularly attended the Orleans AA meeting and gave him a call. He lived in Oxford where Steve had spent his last night out from hell a few months earlier. Steve, once again, took that long twelve-mile drive across gravel roads for a critical visit with Wayne. Two hours later, Steve returned home and poured what little CC was left down the drain.

"Bombshell tonight, friends!" as infamous prosecutor and television personality Nancy Grace would say: As of June 24, 1998, Steve has not tasted another drop of alcohol!

"And by the grace of God, it will be my last forever," he said with all the conviction he could muster.

Had Susan not taken such a bold stand, Steve doubted that he would have gotten back on track. Some might call what she did "tough love". That may be true he said, but nothing in her voice that day sounded like love! As it turns out, he refocused and attended over twenty meetings in the next month. He insists that he owes his life to Susan.

A frequent saying in AA is: "One drink is too many and a thousand not enough."

Here is an analogy that Steve has stated at dozens of meetings over the years: "An AA meeting is like an orgy. You leave feeling much better than when you arrived, but you're not sure who was responsible."

Remember that cup Steve didn't want to "decorate up"? It became much more meaningful with time. It had been over six years between his second trip through Valley Hope and when he landed his last rehab in Minnesota. While there, Steve received a get-well card from Carol, the counselor during both Valley Hope rehabs. She had heard he was trying again and wanted to wish him well. She also said that she had retrieved his cup again and would love to give it to him when he hit one year of sobriety.

Steve achieved his first year of sobriety in the summer of 1999 but didn't believe that he deserved the cup yet. He waited until he had two full years under his belt and then went back to Valley Hope to bring it home. Carol was still there, and she was able to present the cup over a decade after he so grudgingly worked it up the first time he was there in 1989. He never imagined that cup would become as meaningful as it did and the fact that Carol kept pulling it off the shelf before heading to the dumpster two different times made it especially meaningful.

She must have seen something in Steve Knuth from the very beginning that led her to believe he would someday arrive.

CHAPTER 12

SEEDS OF SUCCESS

As a teenager living with an alcoholic, I tried to put the psychological puzzle together of what was happening in our household on a daily basis. I learned that addiction—in basic terms—is mental and physiological. You can pick your poison and sometimes it may be extreme (just watch an episode of "My Strange Addiction"), but habits, associations, and attachments are in the mental realm.

There is fierce debate on addiction being a disease or the lazy person's way out of life's circumstances, problems, and decisions. When you are in the thick of seeing your parent passed out in the front yard on display for the neighbors to see, or simply starving for your parent's attention as Steve's kids were, it doesn't matter if addiction was disease or conscious decision. Needs aren't being fulfilled. Responsibilities go down the drain with the puke from a hangover.

My dad has been dead since 1994. He died in his sleep in the next room from me, and I was nineteen years old when I found him that morning and went to my Shakespearean lit class in a surreal state of delayed response. All these years later, it was absolutely refreshing to have frank conversations with Steve, a husband, father, and community leader only a few years younger than my dad had been when he died. Steve had enough distance to consider all the idiosyncrasies and nuances related to addiction. What I wanted to know most was how he managed to keep his business trajectory intact. Yes, there are millions of functional addicts sitting at desks or speaking in boardrooms at this very moment. Still, Steve's many blackouts, even while driving, bouts of alcohol poisoning, and eyeballs on guns and bridges, go beyond the pale. His business sense simply had to be divine intervention!

Also, how did his mind disassociate from alcohol enough to finally get past eight months without the bottle?

As far back as he could remember, Steve always held a job. He would constantly weigh the pros and cons of drinking when he was in between drunken states, sobering up. Months went by in this kind of agony. Then after this last treatment center, driving on the highway between the fertilizer operation and a town to the south, it hit Steve like a ton of bricks that he had not thought about alcohol for at least a day. One whole day.

Holy crap, he thought. *I might have some hope here.*

He held onto that hope. It took about eight months before he was not having a daily mental battle of drinking or not. Steve needed to stay sober long enough to figure out how to live life differently. That first year is a barrage of endless tests—birthdays, holidays, graduations, work events.

"You got to get through all these events sober and then you know you can do this life...sober. You've got to recognize and get past triggers," he explains.

Most successful startup businesses have an owner who has both a passion for what the business offers and the drive to put in a few years of seventy- to eighty-hour weeks to get it off the ground. Steve certainly had the passion for commodities. However, his "whatever it takes" drive was born out of fear.

Both excitement and fear drove the front end of what would become his company, AgWest Commodities, but fear was the major motivator. To understand this, it is important to understand where Steve was in life, where he was in his journey of living life sober. He had struggled with alcohol for twenty-seven years and it took three rehabs over a ten-year span of time to achieve one full year of abstinence and recovery. He knew he couldn't stay in the stress of the fertilizer and chemical business with any hope remaining sober, and his love of commodities provided some logic to attempt making a living in the brokerage business.

Steve's fear of failure came from more than one direction. He had pitched the idea of opening a brokerage to various people that he respected and although no one flat out told him he was stark raving mad, he doesn't remember anyone who provided strong encouragement of this being a good idea either. The general lack of enthusiasm added to Steve's fear, but was also a benefit because of an "I'll show you" attitude that can show its head.

The fear was even more pronounced when considering Steve was launching AgWest only three days before his first-year anniversary of sobriety. He was, at best, still on shaky ground concerning the drinking. Failure on the sobriety front would assure failure of the new company.

In reflection, the additional fear of not only failing once again on the drinking front but adding to that, a failed business, may have been exactly the added incentive to stay sober that Steve needed at that dicey point in time. It was a bit like one pushing all their remaining chips into the card game...it was an all-in type of bet. It was going to either work or be an epic failure that would have likely sealed Steve's fate of an early death.

Talk about a risk-taking attitude!

Steve made the biggest bet in his life by taking the plunge into AgWest because failure would have been the man's complete undoing. At that shaky point in his life, Steve was betting on himself. It's worth stating that through the writing of this book, this is absolutely a new realization to Steve. He's pretty shocked that he would have or could have rolled that big of a dice...the "life or death" dice.

Growth at AgWest happened immediately and by the end of year two, the company had more employees than he ever imagined. They were having a ball and the business model showed exciting possibilities, but his fear was actually increasing. They were bringing on three or four new employees a year, who were typically the main breadwinners of their families. Steve's fear of failure was now getting extended into multiple families and that responsibility was always on his mind. Many of the first dozen employees took a cut in pay to be a part of AgWest—the idea of letting them down with a failed business model was something Steve hoped he would never have to face. Back to the previous revolution about the size of bet he was making, he simply cannot imagine how he could have lived through a failed AgWest.

Also, in reflection while doing this book, Steve was both amazed and extremely humbled when he thought about the first eight to ten folks that joined the team. Virtually all of them started with less income than at their previous employment. Being a commission-based business model, they obviously felt the upside outweighed the front-end cut. That's the logical side of things, but what struck Steve while rethinking the early years was why all those folks would have placed a bet on their livelihood based on someone so early in recovery. They knew his past. It was no secret. His only answer is that they obviously didn't realize he was still working at navigating a new and very unfamiliar life.

The company's business model is contingent on two streams of revenue. AgWest Commodities is a brokerage firm providing price risk management tools to agricultural producers of soybeans, corn, wheat, cattle and hogs. Via futures and options, they assist farmers in hedging their commodities and the company gets paid a commission every time their clients make a trade. In 2002, the company added a program called Revenue and Profit Management (RPM). The AgWest brokers get to know their customers' operation and goals. They help them come to grips with the cost of production for their farm. It's hard to figure out what price you need if you don't know a baseline of costs. Once this foundation is established, the brokers then help folks build a plan to market their grain. The current market structure provides a logical estimation of what one might expect for an upcoming market range, which is foundational information in building the plans.

The RPM program goes a step further than the competitors in this industry, as they take "power of attorney" to sell their client's production. Basically, AgWest takes on the responsibility of executing the plan. If the market allows the right prices, AgWest triggers the sales to get things done. It is a unique model. The growth has been tremendous. In 2019, AgWest sold 140 million bushels of grain on behalf of its clients.

AgWest Commodities assists nearly 2,500 grain and livestock producers across the Western Corn Belt in managing their commodity price risk through structured plans based on profitability. Unlike most of their competition, AgWest has a philosophical approach that revolves around disciplined plans and recognizing that protecting (not predicting) prices is how folks can market their production with the most consistent profitability.

Steve's self-taught knowledge and acumen culminated into a service recognizing that while farmers are good at growing a crop, many struggle with selling it. Whether they need help creating a marketing plan and executing the actual sale, navigating the many tools available to manage risk or managing the stress that comes with it all, the AgWest team serves as a "marketing partner" for producers.

With this premise and promise, the company would eventually expand to ten locations in four Western Corn Belt states.

In the *AA Big Book*, there is a well-known piece on promises. After Steve's third and last treatment, he started listening to this particular reading and hanging onto it with a sliver of hope. Damned if it didn't all come true!

If we are painstaking about this phase of our development, we will be amazed before we are halfway through. We are going to know a new freedom and a new happiness. We will not regret the past nor wish to shut the door on it. We will comprehend the word serenity and we will know peace. No matter how far down the scale we have gone, we will see how our experience can benefit others. That feeling of uselessness and self-pity will disappear. We will lose interest in selfish things and gain interest in our fellows. Self-seeking will slip away. Our whole attitude and outlook upon life will change. Fear of people and of economic insecurity will leave us. We will intuitively know how to handle situations which used to baffle us. We will suddenly realize that God is doing for us what we could not do for ourselves. Are these extravagant promises? We think not. They are being fulfilled among us—sometimes quickly, sometimes slowly. They will always materialize if we work for them.

CHAPTER 13

DANGEROUS TEST OF SOBRIETY AND SANITY

October 16th was a beautiful fall day in Nebraska that morphed into an equally beautiful evening with clear skies and a light breeze with seasonal temperatures in the fifties. This is harvest time in the Corn Belt and on evenings like this, the countryside is dotted with lights into the 10:00-to-midnight hours as folks take advantage of the weather and push to harvest the annual corn and soybean crops.

Susan's daughter, Julie, was a freshman in high school playing in a freshman and sophomore tournament at Southern Valley, a consolidated school like many in rural Nebraska. The dwindling rural population has forced consolidation to the point that each little town could no longer educate kids on an economy of scale. Southern Valley sits in the country between the three towns that closed schools to become part of the new consolidated system. Those three towns are Beaver City, Orleans (remember, the town of 300 people and some vacant meth houses), and Oxford, where Steve graduated from high school in 1971.

Due to Julie's game being a tournament, the start time was early so Susan and Steve left work together in her car at about 5:00 to head cross-country to Southern Valley. Alma, the school Julie attended, was scheduled to play in the first game and then again, in the last game of the evening. Julie was a freshman and to that point in the school year, had seen little game time. She didn't play much in the first game but was involved quite a lot in the last game they played. She did well, including a couple of ace serves, and Susan was thrilled. Susan loved volleyball and had herself been a force in high school, so she wanted Julie to do well and experience the excitement she had enjoyed in her day.

Susan was thrilled about Julie's performance, chatting about it on the twenty-five-minute drive back to the office. This fact eliminates any thoughts (some had) that she fell asleep on her drive home. They arrived back at the office at 9:30. Steve had driven home so he got out and Susan slipped into the driver's seat to make the seven-mile drive to her home in Huntly, Nebraska.

Steve went in the house and did what he did every evening—turned the TV on for background noise and went to work on his computer. You already know he was a real night owl back then! He never really got out of the late-night mode after he quit drinking either. His employees would often joke about the 1:00 to 3:00 a.m. emails they would receive. For the longest time, he had an enormous amount of guilt that he was sitting there on a computer sending work-related emails while Susan was pinned in her car and dying just three miles south of him.

Two hours after Susan backed out of the driveway, Steve's doorbell rang. No one wants a visitor at your door near midnight, as nothing good comes with late night calls or doorbells. When Steve opened the door and saw the sheriff, he immediately thought something had happened to his son, Jamie, who drove a truck at the time. The officer asked to come in. They walked a few steps up to the living room and he informed Steve that Susan was in a wreck by the Huntly spur, just three miles south. She didn't survive.

With life knocked out of him, Steve slumped over the stair railing.

After a long pause, the sheriff asked if Steve could help find their way to Susan's brothers' farms, about ten miles across country roads, to deliver the news to them. She had four brothers. Four stops.

In slow motion, Steve got dressed and jumped in his truck, wondering if this were just a nightmare. He didn't drink anymore. He had not blacked out.

First came Susan's youngest brother, Chris's house. Then Dennis, the oldest. By then, Steve couldn't go any further. He couldn't say or hear the news of Susan, his love, the woman he hoped to marry, being dead in the middle of the night. He headed back home and vividly remembers thinking to himself that no one was going to blame him if he drank. Most would assume this outcome anyway, right? If he ever needed an excuse, this would be it. Fortunately, those thoughts lasted only a couple of minutes.

Steve called his sponsor, Keith. He didn't tell him on the phone what was going on but urged that he needed to visit and asked if he would put on some coffee.

The twenty-minute drive from Susan's family to Keith and Delores's house was completely surreal. Steve kept thinking that maybe this really was just a horrendous dream. When he arrived at their place, it fully sunk in that he was awake, and that Susan was gone. He stayed with them for three hours before heading back home. Steve had been sober just over five years at that point. This is how powerful the sponsorship in AA can be.

Keith reminded him that Susan had been there when he accepted his five-year medallion. He had heard other people say, "Year five is a tough one." When accepting his five-year coin, he spoke to the group about how difficult the past year had been for him. Today, he doesn't even remember why it was so difficult but absolutely remembers talking about it on his fifth birthday AA meeting. He told them that he hoped year "6" would be better. That was in July of 2003, just over three months before Susan's death. Odds did not favor him reaching his next sobriety birthday.

Keep in mind that Steve is the guy who never wanted a sponsor. Through the early years, Keith became his sponsor, mentor, and best friend in sobriety. Besides Susan, Keith was the most instrumental person in Steve a path to finding recovery.

The details of Susan's accident unfolded. She had hit a semi head-on. The skid marks from her vehicle, which was only six months old, showed that she had lost control and crossed the centerline. Was it a deer? Another animal she swerved to miss? A bee in the car? Something unexpected happened on that drive and to this day, no one knows what. Steve had to give up his inquiry months later, or he would have driven himself insane. It was already unbearable losing both a business partner and significant other.

Another aspect of the accident that was difficult for Steve was the physical markings left on the highway that indicated to even the uniformed passerby that something atrocious had happened. One could almost reenact the event by the skid marks from both Susan's car and those left by the truck after impact, along with stains of vehicle fluids where Susan's car came to a stop right in the center of the highway. Steve traveled that stretch of highway multiple times a week and it was more than a year later when the state resurfaced Highway 183, covering the evidence of a tragedy.

The summer following the accident, Steve created a memorial adjacent to where Susan's car came to a stop. For hours, by himself, he carried concrete blocks and a five-foot steel cross that Susan's son, Steven, built. He had to tote all the materials into a tree grove to reach an opening between two cedars that faced the highway. It was a sizable project for one individual, but Steve needed that time to reflect; this became part of his grieving process. He built the memorial to last and it remains in good shape today. It is a peaceful place to leave flowers during Memorial Day weekend and on the anniversary of that awful night.

With all the "bullshit things" he had done in his life, Steve felt buried in a pile of survivor's guilt. He had driven tens of thousands of miles drunk. Why was this kind of crash not his cross to bear? There is no doubt that Steve had a purpose to be here. It also drives him to give back.

In reflection, Steve didn't realize until the writing of his story how influential females have been in his life.

Most folks didn't go skipping into the AA rooms with a smile on their face and feeling glad to be there. In fact, most or all didn't want anything to do with the meetings or the people in the meetings. They went because they were out of options. They went because their cycle of abuse no longer served them.

Through the first two attempts at sobriety, Steve never got comfortable with the meetings. He wouldn't say much and tried to be as invisible as possible due to shame and simply not wanting to accept that he was like these folks. Many who Steve got to know in those early AA meetings seemed settled and even happy, which was a foreign concept to him. There is a saying in AA: "You should go to meetings until you want to go to meetings." How simple is that? The problem is, Steve never believed he could actually get to a time when he would desire attending a meeting.

In the spring of 1998 and still feeling uncomfortable in meetings, his daughter, Ronda, lived just three miles away. One night, they were having supper at her place. Steve was leaving from there for a meeting in Orleans and jokingly asked Kiley, his three-year-old granddaughter, if she wanted to go. She was so excited her grandpa asked her to go somewhere with him that he couldn't retract!

What he found by accident was the folks at the meeting just loved her and the most important thing was all eyes were on her and not Steve. He asked his sponsor if he thought bringing this adorable three-year-old was a problem and Keith said no. Kiley became Steve's AA meeting comrade for several years. Just her very presence became such a buffer for him and took the edge off of what irked him about meetings in the first place—awkwardness, visibility, shame.

Kiley attended approximately 200 meetings with her grandfather. By the time she reached the age of 5 or 6, Keith explained to Steve that some folks may feel uncomfortable saying what they needed to say with someone that age in the room. By that time, something unexpected had happened. He actually got to a point that he *wanted* to go to meetings.

Steve used to joke that if Kiley ever got *mipped* (or found to be possessing alcohol as a minor) in high school and the judge sent her to AA (which happens regularly) that she would have no problem carrying out the order. She would just be getting reacquainted with all her old friends!

Now twenty-four years old and a gifted musician in two professional bands, Kiley rarely drinks. For that, Steve is exceptionally grateful.

CHAPTER 14

A NEW DAY
FOR CHANGE

Steve had lost his life partner and business partner in one fatal crash. He became so cognizant that all of it can be over in a millisecond. It changes you when someone so dear to you that suddenly dies.

He was more determined to live better, not simply "not drink." There's truly so much to life. Steve was not college educated, but he has an IQ that is above average. People that are smarter than average tend to have more trouble getting sober; they try to figure out how to do this on their own. Well, Steve finally figured out that IQ was no match for addiction.

What Steve did need the IQ for was saving his business after Susan, who had been the operational fabric of AgWest for the past few years, died. He was fortunate enough to have a team of business saviors and loyal clients surrounding him. To this day, they are all a tight-knit ag family.

Carrie Trompke, who had been answering phones, stepped in to learn and direct finances. Carrie grew up on a family farm north of Loomis and is a graduate of the University of Nebraska. She has a solid understanding of agriculture, but the company's financial affairs and overseeing risk management seemed rather outlandish at the time.

In her words: "I interviewed with him and Susan on a Saturday morning. He offered me a job. Susan passed away a year later, and the company needed someone in her role. He put so much trust in me, supported my learning curve, and listened to my fears. Steve asks a lot of questions and he is invested in the person he is talking to; he doesn't pry for information, but he really wants to engage. Three years later, he hired my husband as a broker.

"The morning that Susan died, it was one of those mornings you never forget. I passed a roadblock right at the intersection to Steve's house... AgWest. The highway headed south from the office was closed, which seemed very unusual. What I didn't know is the authorities were still processing the accident site from the night before.

"I was always the first one to work, turning on the lights and making the first of many pots of coffee for the day. Steve came downstairs and I was shocked to see him awake. In a painfully low voice, he told me that

Susan had been killed in a car crash. Two days prior, he had announced that she had taken half ownership of the company. Over the course of that week, there were numerous conversations in his living room about the business and why this had happened, why she crossed into the wrong lane. Why? He wanted to know so badly. He searched for answers and then he stayed involved with Susan's kids. She had helped him turn his life around. He would not have let her down for the world. I think this carried over after her death. I felt guilty though because a horrible situation turned into a unique opportunity for me. I had a chance to step into another position. I was raised on a farm. I understood ag, but markets, no. I went to school to be a math teacher! People we hire haven't necessarily been in this field before, but they have to understand who we work with: producers. They're hardworking to the bone, good people. We do the right thing here, not the easy road. We treat others with respect. Steve's huge on customer service. Put the customer first."

Paul Mussman joined the AgWest team just three months after Susan's death. Paul was in the Army reserves and had just returned home after an eighteen-month deployment in Afghanistan and then he was involved in the invasion of Iraq to overthrow the government of Saddam Hussein. Paul had taken a commodities class while in college at Fort Hays State and knew he wanted to be in that business. The position he was interviewing for was the one Carrie had performed for a year before Susan died. He started out answering phones as an insanely overqualified veteran. Paul is now president of the company.

"In 2003, I was in the Army and had overseas experience with deployments in Afghanistan, Iraq, and Qatar. After being gone for eighteen months, I wanted to be in commodities. I answered an ad and interviewed with Steve. Two days later, he interviewed me. Those days, we all answered the phone. He slept, ate and worked upstairs in his home. The morning I interviewed with him, he was very professional. The office smelled like smoke. I had this picture of a Chicago trader with bourbon and cigars. That is what the stockbrokers did. Steve wasn't far off that image. Once I started, I saw him in a robe a couple of times wanting coffee. The first issue I had with him was that I didn't make the coffee strong enough! In his low but firm voice, he said, 'If you're going to put the effort into it, make it stronger.' Back then, everything was by fax, colored highlighters and pencils.

"In twenty years, there have been big obstacles. The switch to electronic trading when we had to tell the guys they couldn't talk and shout to the traders in Chicago. They had to move to computers. The original AgWest office was Steve's house, which was located ten miles from the closest town. Rural America was not well-connected, and some costly provisions were made to operate in this new and quickly changing electronic world. Every mile, (ten miles to Alma), we had booster boxes for dialing up the Internet over one of our phone connections. We would see these white vans rolling up to check connectivity. Big pain. We lost electricity for two weeks due to a horrific ice storm. Steve jumped in his Suburban on a Saturday night, drove to Des Moines, Iowa, to get a generator to keep us going. He pulled a small trailer and filled it with generators while there and had most of them sold over the phone by the time he got back. We set up a decent-sized generator to run the office and Steve lined up a farmer to come by with fuel every day. He has people here that would lay down their lives for him.

"How do I measure my own success? Doing something innovative. Then you get to know the customers. Then their families. You have your own family. I hope this doesn't get to be the biggest company. I don't want to be overly successful and forget where we are from."

Besides Susan, Jim Engler was Steve's first employee. He has worked for several of the Knuths' family businesses for forty years and has been there to see Steve's evolution.

"I didn't want to get into the fertilizer business but when TriCo, Dewey's company, bought out the grain facility where I was working, Steve talked me into sticking around. That was back in the early 1980s. I visited him at Valley Hope a couple of times. He was in denial about the scope of his addiction. Steve and I both like technical analysis of markets, drawing lines on charts and studying various market indicators. When he decided to leave Cargill and go fulltime with the brokerage business, the thought of joining his new venture was intriguing. I was going to take a pay cut in working for him, not to mention the fact that this gentleman was just coming out of rehab. But he was so trustworthy! He was always thinking of ideas toward helping farmers with their marketing. I saw a kind, smart man with a lot of great ideas. That is why I took the leap of faith and joined Steve and Susan at AgWest.

"I struggled with the same issues as farmers—trying to figure out markets and developing the right price risk management strategy. The farmer is always trying to determine where to sell his product. Unfortunately, in the world of a farmer, you have a lot of things affecting your bottom line: weather, government, and life events. A patchwork of decisions and emotions. If grain prices are not good, it generally means the world is producing too much. Marketing is difficult; it is a psychological struggle to deal with so much uncertainty.

"The central question the business solves for: How can we help control the emotions using marketing tools that will allow farmers to weather difficult times without panic and starvation, using futures and options? The key thing we do for our clients is helping them control emotions that can destroy the best of marketing plans. There is a lot that goes into developing a plan including the tools of our trade, futures and options but the real key is helping folks remain disciplined to execute the plan as designed. It sounds so simple, but it can easily be complicated by emotions run amuck.

"We are successful because of Steve and a lot of the people here. For farmers, the money they receive from selling their production pays off debt, upgrades tractors and combines, puts food on their tables and pays for medical insurance, doctor and hospital bills and anything else the average person needs for a comfortable living. Selling when markets are providing opportunity can make a $200,000 difference for an average-size operation. Sound marketing can be the difference in the survival of an operation.

The outside world, the city folks, sees shiny equipment and can easily make the assumption that farming is a cash cow. Well, to some degree that would be right because it doesn't take much of an operation to have over a million dollars in gross revenue each year, but what they may not understand is that it takes a pile of money to grow that crop. Farming is laced with uncertainty!"

Finally, one of Steve's good friends that helped him formulate his philosophical approach to production marketing is Jim Hodge. After receiving his bachelor's degree from the University of Nebraska, Jim became the fourth-generation operator of their family's farm. Over time, Jim developed a disciplined approach to marketing that has worked well for his operation and he's now offering years of trading experience and a rock-solid discipline to assist other producers in successfully marketing their production.

"I got all my fertilizer from Steve, as that is how we met so many years ago. I graduated in ag-econ with a business option and came home to run the farm. It started with my great grandfather. My son is the fifth generation. We've farmed in Harlan County for 100 years. My grandmother was born in 1902. She lived in a sod house [a rectangular dwelling with walls built of sod or turf bricks, laid in horizontal layers with small windows, and a roof covered with earthen sods or thatch] for a couple of years. My grandpa, Holly Sr., came over from Sweden and lived a couple miles cross-country and they got married. They built a house south of town and my son lives in it today with his family. Farming was a great way to raise kids.

"In the 1980s, we had 18-20% interest rates. It was hard to make enough money. The interest was a big weight. Prices weren't good enough to make up that difference. We tried to hang onto the assets we had. We haven't had 18% interest since then. My grandparents lived twelve miles south of town. There were no roads, so they rode on top of ridges. They were raising chickens and milking cows for cream. Grandma told me they would get in their wagon once a week, ride it with the eggs and cream, and take it to the railroad track where the creamery was located and sell it. This was an all-day event. This is how they paid off their farm.

"One day, they were riding into town in the wagon and a guy was walking along. She offered him a ride to Holdrege, and he said, 'Well, I'm in a hurry so I need to walk.' Sure enough, he beat them to Holdrege! When they were able to move to a bigger place, they picked up that sod house and a couple of steam engines and moved it all to their land. Holly Jr., my dad, farmed with his dad. We are currently farming 3,000 acres of corn and soybeans. When the Hodge family started farming, this was mostly wheat country."

As a little context to Jim's mentioning of high interest rates in the 80s, a Midwestern farm crisis ravaged the nation as the result of the economy slumping, foreign markets drying up and debts piling up. Thousands of families lost their farms. Many sold their land and simply vanished. Land values dropped 55 percent between 1982 and 1987 in Nebraska.

CHAPTER 15

LANGUAGE OF THE STRAINED HEART

After Susan's death in the fall of 2003, Steve spent several months dealing with survivor guilt and trying to figure out what his life looked like going forward. Some would say it was too early, but he started dating about eight months after Susan's death. He was lost and alone. Would I be wrong to say that men generally don't do very well with solitude? This has always been Steve's case.

Steve started dating someone from AA and that blew up into an absolute disaster. It thankfully ended in only a few weeks. About a year after Susan's death, another woman called him who he had admired from afar for many years. She was nineteen years his junior. In fact, Steve had presented her 8th grade diploma when he was president of the small school system that she attended. They spent hours on the phone, as she was fresh off a divorce and didn't want the general public to know that she was actively dating. This went on for several weeks and they were only face to face a couple of times through that period. Steve was in such a vulnerable state that it was easy to fall head over heels for this gorgeous, young woman who he had always admired. What he didn't realize was, there was more to her story about not wanting to go public. At the same time they were talking, she was reviving a high school relationship with a man who was also recently divorced. By the time this became evident, Steve had fallen hook, line and sinker for her. It was devastating.

Here, Steve was sixteen months after losing Susan and going through another heart-wrenching loss. As with so many things in his life, it took him some time to realize he had actually dodged a bullet. Had their relationship developed into something long-term, she may have been his eventual undoing concerning sobriety.

A few weeks later, Steve and Jan had their first date. They had known each other from ten years earlier, and he had his eye on her. She didn't show much interest in him back then and as he found out on their first date, she thought maybe he drank too much...imagine that!

It was a first date that came close to never happening. Steve had decided to subscribe to a month of the dating site, Match.com, and the first person that caught his eye was the very attractive gal living just ten miles from his house. Jan's profile picture displayed her petting a live tiger while laying down facing the camera. Talk about catching your eye. Steve did not recognize her when he reached out to see if she had any interest in meeting. The reason the first date came close to never happening is because the day Steve contacted her on Match, she had also planned to let the subscription lapse. Would they have ever crossed paths otherwise?

On that terrific first date, Steve and Jan talked for hours like they had known each other forever. He discovered that she had her own struggles. She had been in an abusive marriage for ten years right out of high school and following that, she had to work herself through a difficult breakup with a guy who she adored. She ended that relationship because he had developed a meth addiction. Although never addicted to drugs or alcohol herself, she knew and understood recovery principles better than Steve. That was a very positive component to this new relationship. Jan had gone through a great deal of self-help, including an in-depth course by Dr. Phil. She pulled herself together both psychologically and financially, coming off of that bad deal by the time Steve met her several years later. Because of her past, she understood addiction and the principles of effective programs, including Al-Anon. How could these unique skills and experiences not serve their relationship?

Steve realized in short order that Jan was one of the strongest women he had ever known. She knew who she was and what she wanted. Her strength and her refusal to take any bullshit off of anyone was exactly what a six-year recovering alcoholic needed. Steve wouldn't call it "love at first sight," but it did not take them long to know this was real and that they could become outstanding partners to face life's challenges together.

Their first date was in early February 2005. They were engaged by July and married in November of 2005. She came into Steve's life at a critically important time. Jan is undoubtedly one of those important women in Steve's life.

"God willing, she will be the last that I need," he said.

CHAPTER 16

STEVE'S SURRENDER

The process of recovery can use every meaningful mantra or message it can get. The following verse in the *Bible* is referring to children of Israel who had circled a mountain in the desert for over thirty years, but the words are also a fitting metaphor for the moment an addict surrenders.

Deuteronomy 2:2-3: "You were made for more than to be stuck in a vicious cycle of defeat. You have circled this mountain long enough. Now turn north."

With surrender came immense growth. Steve had started the business in his home and once he had ten employees, there was not one room that wasn't bustling with activity. They were practically busting through the walls. Before they moved to a real office, they joked that the next employee would have a desk in one of the bathrooms.

Paul talked about making the coffee too weak. Carrie talked about taking the dog out fifty times a day. This is significant in that it's humbling to think of those days when they were hard-pressed to get to the washroom because it was wall-to-wall people. At the same time, they operated like a family in that house, setting the stage for the level of intimacy they have with their 2,500 clients.

AgWest grew in trading volume to be in the top 5 percent of agriculture brokers in the country. Steve had assumed his basement would work forever! His goal had been for him and Susan to "scrape a living out of this thing." He aspired to get 250 clients, which seemed fantastical in and of itself. Through surrender, Steve paved the way to blossom into a real leader. In tandem with navigating addiction, he has learned numerous invaluable lessons.

In the earlier years, when he tried to bring a new initiative to this organization, Steve figured out the hard way that you better make sure you have buy-in through the ranks. He invested in a tech company that he thought had developed a product AgWest could utilize for their customer base. It didn't work. None of the brokers wanted the changes and Steve didn't do due diligence to test it and gain consensus.

Thereafter, he amplified his communication with employees and clients.

Every week, the company puts out a five-minute read that Steve writes. It's designed to be motivational, inspirational and informative. He does all of the signature writing and half of the speaking. Paul also does quite a lot of speaking. From fall harvest to spring planting, the pair splits up about forty presentations. (Needless to say, Steve drives a lot of icy roads in the winter!)

From early on when the employee count started to grow, Steve put out a weekend internal memo. It was a short read that shared with employees the company's initiatives, specifics on markets and program directives and anything else he felt may be of interest. He was diligent with this task and estimates he only missed a handful of weekend memos over the years. "When we started opening branch offices and the entire team no longer operated shoulder to shoulder, the memo served to keep everyone on a same page...everyone hitched to the same wagon."

For these presentations, Steve was in Iowa for six weeks straight in the winter of 2018-2019, one of the coldest on record. It was brutally cold. Still, Steve loves to educate and engage audiences. He's done a thousand hour-long seminars for this business. He didn't flourish as a speaker overnight though.

Steve's first presentations for his new company were awful. As that kid in a class of about thirty-five kids, he froze up in high school doing a book report because he hadn't read the book. The memory of that humiliation stuck with him and he avoided all public speaking until he started AgWest. Steve's two brothers did not mind speaking, so he was not required to handle those duties throughout the years in the fertilizer business.

Steve recalls doing an introduction of a chemical representative to a small group of farmers, probably no more than a dozen. He lost his train of thought and froze, froze like an icicle. Throughout his life's struggles he was always searching for answers to get better. He had acquired quite a library of self-help books and CDs, including a series by Tony Robbins. From one of Tony's CDs, Steve picked up a one-liner that was instrumental in helping him get through the front end of his speaking career: "Feel the fear and do it anyway." As silly as it may sound, Steve would get by himself before speaking (usually in his car to have one last cigarette) and literally repeat that line over and over, "Feel the fear and do it anyway." He remembers nothing else of the Tony Robins motivational tapes, but that one line made all the difference in the early days of AgWest.

As he reminisced about the early fears, he acknowledged that he probably owes Tony Robbins something.

Steve knew that if he wanted to grow his business, he needed to get better in front of a crowd. He went to a three-day Dale Carnegie class on high-impact speaking. That was the most grueling thing he ever put himself through—aside of rehabs and AA meetings. However, it did him so much good that a year later, he participated in the same event. Since then, he has done hundreds of educational and market updates in promoting AgWest and has served as a guest speaker at various Bankers Association conventions.

Public speaking is the biggest surprise concerning the history of AgWest. Steve was the typical individual when it comes to speaking; death offered a better alternative than getting in front of a crowd. He moved from an overwhelming fear to presentations becoming the most enjoyable aspect of the business. The strangest aspect of this transformation may be that he likes a big crowd...the bigger the crowd, the better.

Steve feeds off the energy in the room now. In a recent Nebraska Bankers Association event with seven other speakers, 130 ag lenders attended and rated Steve Knuth as one of the top speakers.

Steve's involvement and outreach does not stop at a podium. For the man that never sleeps, he's always in motion for greater good.

For example, Valley Hope is spread over seven states with multiple treatment centers. Its mission reads as follows: *Valley Hope will provide a quality continuum of comprehensive treatment and related services, in a caring atmosphere and at a reasonable price for all people experiencing problems with alcohol and other drug use.*

The reason this is so important to Steve is that he wanted to return something to Valley Hope. To return as the man he is without the bottle and to give back. He's been on the Foundation Board for eleven years and on the main Valley Hope Association board for three years and currently serves as vice chair of that board. The Valley Hope foundation stays near the top of Steve and Jan's philanthropy list. In 2018 and early 2019, the board functioned at the top of the organization of over 600 employees for nine months while they were without a CEO.

In his position, one of the things on his bucket list was to spearhead the building of a recovery-meeting house in Holdrege. Meetings right now are either in the basement of a church or the back room of the coffee shop. If there was a place specifically for this purpose, Steve felt there would certainly be more meetings available to folks and with much improved quality as well.

That said, in the fall of 2018, Steve finally put the thought into action. He reached out to a number of recovering folks and a couple of key individuals in the community to serve on a new non-profit board. They organized under the name of South Central Area Recovery, which is a cool name because of the acronym it allows them to ear-tag the organization as SCAR. SCAR seems appropriate for the folks this project will serve.

One of the board members is a woman in recovery who works for a legal firm in town. Mindi has been extremely instrumental in getting all the necessary paperwork and filings in place to establish a 501c non-profit. They were granted non-profit status in the summer of 2019, which allowed them to be one of the eighty non-profits listed in the Phelps County Foundation's annual Give-Day. Steve's goal for SCAR on that day was to land in the top five of the eighty or so no-profits listed in 2019. As a county, the $882,000 for the day broke the previous year's record. But what was most astounding is that SCAR not only topped all the non-profits in the area; it raised $180,000 on the day. That spoke volumes of how the community feels about the project. The SCAR board is now hopeful that ground will be broken on the $600,000 project over the next year.

The first thing that Steve did to show his gratitude when he received the incredible news was review and celebrate the "promises" found in the *AA Big Book*:

1.   If we are painstaking about this phase of our development, we will be amazed before we are halfway through. This promise states that people who complete the AA program and make a sincere effort will begin to see changes in their lives even before they are halfway done.

2.   We are going to know a new freedom and a new happiness. People who finish the steps will experience

relief from the suffering of addiction and feel free to pursue a new life without alcohol.

3.   We will not regret the past nor wish to shut the door on it. Those who work the program will gain a sense of acceptance that allows them to process their experiences, learn from them, and move on without guilt.

4.   We will comprehend the word serenity, and we will know peace. Addiction can lead to a constant state of inner turmoil. The AA program helps people find a calmness that is rare during active using, and that many addicts have never known in their lives.

5.   No matter how far down the scale we have gone, we will see how our experience can benefit others. Many addicts don't believe that other people understand what they've been through. But in AA, they often meet people who can identify with and learn from their experiences.

6.   That feeling of uselessness and self-pity will disappear. Addiction makes users feel worthless and guilty about their actions. The steps can give people a sense that their lives have a meaning and a purpose, particularly through helping others.

7.   We will lose interest in selfish things and gain interest in our fellows. Addiction leads to many self-centered behaviors. Helping other people find recovery can

bring addicts outside of themselves and help them develop a genuine interest in other people.

8. Self-seeking will slip away. The tunnel vision of focusing only on oneself and drinking usually begins to fade as people work the steps.

9. Our whole attitude and outlook upon life will change. AA can shift one's perspective from hopeless to hope. People can begin to imagine a life where they are happy.

10. Fear of people and of economic insecurity will leave us. Alcoholics who recover through AA don't feel like they have to hide anymore or worry about how to support their addiction and maintain financial security.

11. We will intuitively know how to handle situations, which used to baffle us. As the AA member gets deeper into the recovery process, they begin to see situations more clearly and can tap into their inner resources.

12. We will suddenly realize that God is doing for us what we could not do for ourselves. The concept of a higher power is central to AA. This higher power, be it God or something else, becomes a guiding force in the person's life.

For the past twenty years, Steve has implemented the twelve steps faithfully. Perhaps the one I can most relate to as a non-alcoholic though acutely aware that promises (or sacred contracts) are essential to making life worthwhile and dignified, is No. 5., giving back.

And there must be something about the number, forty, as Steve has a lot of friends that have been with him for over forty years, not to mention that blackjack stint of forty hours! Jeff Swanson has been a friend and client of Steve's for, well, forty years.

It seems that every community in rural America has a family or two with a fighting reputation. Not that these young men go looking, but they are quick to let fists and boots rather than words settle disagreements. The Swanson clan is one of those families. Jeff has a lot of scars, mostly farm-related accidents but no doubt, some from his younger days when settling disagreements. Steve had informed me about the upper body strength Jeff possesses. One evening back in the 1980s, Steve made a smart-assed comment to Jeff, who was on the other side of a near chest-high counter at the fertilizer plant. Jeff reached across the two-foot surface and picked Steve up, all 200 pounds of him, and pulled him up on the countertop.

Jeff's strength could get him in trouble. And several years ago, he reached out to stop a calf that was running right past him and he got the calf stopped but snapped a tendon loose from his shoulder in the process. Just another one of several surgery scars.

Another family with the fighting gene was the Hammonds. They came from the next county south where Steve managed the fertilizer plant. Butch Hammond was a loyal employee of Steve's for many years at TriCo. Age and wisdom had slowed him by the time Steve got to know Butch, but one of his distinguishing features was a missing finger. At a much younger age, he lost the finger in a bar fight. The guy he was fighting bit it off at the knuckle. As the story goes, Butch still ended up getting the best of the guy before he and his buddy drove an hour back to his hometown that night. He went to bed with his hand wrapped in towels and waited until morning to see a doctor. These rare families with reputations are just a cut above in the tough category.

Now, Steve and Jeff got acquainted in the early 1980s when Jeff was starting to put together a farming operation. Jeff leaned on Steve as a sounding board for ideas well beyond fertilizer decisions and they became good friends. Jeff didn't drink as often as Steve, but there were occasions when Jeff would stop by the fertilizer plant and the two of them would have a drink or ten together. He didn't realize that Steve had a real problem. But this is also the "Jeff" who almost took Steve's guns out of the house during his divorce in the late 1980s. Jeff witnessed him get deeper and deeper in the bottle.

During the spring planting season, Steve and Jeff worked horrendous hours, with Jeff getting his crops planted in between tending his cow/calf herd of hundreds and Steve managing the fertilizer plant, along with twenty-five employees under his charge. Jeff remembers one day during a terrible spring, they were each killing themselves to get the work done. Jeff was up early checking fields at 3:00 or 3:30 in the morning to see if the rain that night was enough to stop progress. He ran into Steve at an intersection close to the fertilizer plant. Steve was doing the same thing. That moment in time explained a lot about both of them and the dedication they had to making things happen. They pulled up, side by side, with windows down and just shook their heads at each other. Oh, the insanity of a spring in rural America! In many ways, through those forty years, they have had each other's backs.

When it came time for Jeff's son to escape addiction, Steve had the whole family's back.

While in high school, Zach had a terrible accident and nearly lost a leg. He fell asleep going to football practice on a Saturday morning. He had aspirations to play college football at a Division II level to start, but instead, he endured sixteen surgeries in thirty-five days. With his dream taken away from him, he started self-medicating. He was prescribed all kinds of narcotics for the pain. When Zach hit a wall in the supply, he drank so much to forget about that dream and to the point that alcohol would likely kill him... and it came close to doing just that!

When I was interviewing Jeff for this book, he said that Zach, now 30, had just talked that morning about how Steve helped him to recovery. He had gone to rehab once and it didn't take, and knowing Steve had three rehab trips made it easier for Zack to try again. Steve talked with Zack off and on for three or four years while he was trying—and then not trying—to get sober. Steve happened to be there on a Sunday morning when Zack was ready to go back for another try. He's been sober for more than three years. Zach taught his father that addiction is an everyday struggle.

"Before this miracle, we had found him at his college dorm so far gone, I lost my breath. Steve is our hero for helping him. I don't know that his mother could live through more of what we went through. We needed Steve or someone like him to make a difference. It's human nature to feel self-pity. Steve has gotten up in the middle of the night to drive people to facilities. He supports the community in every way he can."

CHAPTER 17

RESCUING ALL LIVING THINGS

Remember Snoop, the dog? Since he was Steve's best friend during his drinking days, there is simply no telling what that dog witnessed.

For the first five years of Snoop's life, Steve worked across the road from his house at the fertilizer plant. Snoop had free reign of the facility. He would greet everyone in the morning and just mosey around, in and out, all day doing what dogs do. He liked everyone and everyone liked Snoop. He often rode with Steve on errands and field checks. When in Holdrege, Steve would often go through the drive-thru of McDonald's to get Snoop his own plain hamburger. Snoop could have swallowed it whole, but Steve would break it into four bits for him to savor it.

Snoop was the perfect listener. Steve wishes he had a recording of some of those conversations...well, maybe not!

The dog whisperers of Holdrege, Nebraska, Jan and Steve have had dogs all through their fourteen years together. They feel most of them can sense people's moods and that Snoop knew how much Steve was hurting at times.

Steve left for his last rehab on a Monday morning in early February of 1998. It was in Minnesota so he obviously left home headed north. Snoop was a housedog at night, but he could also handle being outside when necessary. For the twenty-six days Steve was gone, Snoop spent his days at the plant with folks he knew and lived outside at night. The folks said that as soon as they started arriving in the morning, Snoop would show up to greet everyone and to get fed. He then spent much of his day laying in the middle of a wide driveway outlining the fertilizer plant. It was a miserable February with blistery cold and often misty conditions. The folks at the plant informed Steve that regardless of the weather, Snoop spent a lot of his day in the middle of the driveway waiting and looking north in the direction that Steve had last gone.

The rehab facility released Steve a day early because they needed his bed. Excited to get home, Steve drove straight through for nine hours and pulled into his driveway at about 5:00 a.m. Snoop went wild like dogs do when you're away.

"You know the reason dogs are better than wives?" Steve quipped. "The later you come home, the happier they are!"

Snoop had always been one to punish Steve when he was away for a few hours or a few days. He would get all wound up like dogs do for just a few minutes and then would go off to a different room in the house and ignore Steve for a few hours. After being gone twenty-six days, Steve didn't expect that would be the case but sure enough, after five minutes or so of extreme excitement, he went to a different room and left him on his own.

Soon after, Steve had a real scare with Snoop. Roger, Steve's friend, wanted to show him something in one of his fields. Snoop always rode in the cab with Steve, but they took Roger's pickup and Steve didn't want to ask him if Snoop could get up front with him. He put Snoop in the back of his pickup, and they headed east on a gravel road. About half mile from the plant a deer ran across the road. They were traveling about fifty miles an hour and Roger had slowed slightly when he saw the deer. Steve looked in his mirror to see if Snoop was all right and at that moment, saw him leap from the pickup to go after the deer.

Snoop rolled multiple times when he landed in the ditch. It was quite a sight with his long legs going every which direction. Steve was sure he would have broken a leg or two, but other than being sore for a few days, Snoopy survived the ordeal. They were both risk-takers!

When Jan and Steve had started dating, she had two dogs of her own. After a few dates, they decided it was time to test the waters, so he brought Snoop along. Things went well for the first time or two but unannounced and unprovoked, Snoop attacked the smallest of the two dogs right in front of them in Jan's living room. It was a little hairy but didn't last long. Then shortly after, he did the same thing with her larger dog, which weighed fifty pounds, about half the size of Snoop. That incident got everyone's attention and as Steve drove home with Snoop that night, he thought that might be the end of his relationship with Jan. She loved her dogs more than anything and if the three of them couldn't be integrated, their relationship wasn't going anywhere.

Fortunately, Snoop walked a straight line after!

In 2007, they were living in Steve's old house where AgWest started because their house in Holdrege sat on blocks while they were digging a basement. Steve was working at the Holdrege house when Jan called to alert Steve that something was wrong with Snoop. He was thirteen at that time, which is rather old for a dog his size. As it turns out, he evidently had a stroke and after three days of nursing and seeing if he was going to come out of it, they had to make the call. Steve didn't cry easily but after everything this furry friend had gone through with him, it was very emotional to say goodbye.

Steve has loved several dogs since Snoop, but none with the same intense bond.

I saw, firsthand, that Steve and Jan are special pet owners. Just as parents talk about their kids in very explicit ways, they talk about the animals in the same vein. The pets have little lives that are intertwined with each other and their owners. In recent years, they have brought elderly and often sickly dogs home from shelters because they have slim odds of being adopted.

Each dog has a pillbox. In 2018, they had to say goodbye to a very special dog, a blue heeler that they brought home as a pup in their first year of marriage. They called her Sidney. She was the most athletic dog either one of them have ever been around. Steve taught Sidney how to play fetch with a tennis ball when she was a pup, and it stuck until the day she died. Sidney had to go outside to play ball three or four times a day, no matter what the weather brought. They would play ball in the middle of a blizzard! It was easy to lose tennis balls in the snow, so keeping spares around was a must. Sidney was Jan's dog all the way and will always have a special place in Jan's heart.

They financially support a rescue in Hastings, Nebraska, and Jan is on the Holdrege Animal Shelter Board. There is a three-dog limit in Holdrege, so they maintain at three and sometimes four, but no one has ever noticed or complained. The health of the rescues varies but back in 2018, they had three dogs, each with medical issues. Their vet bill typically ran $600 to $800 a month during that time.

They currently have three dogs with only one, Lucy, requiring

medication. She is a beautiful Australian Shepard that at age 10, developed diabetes. The owners did not want to deal with her condition and took her to a vet to be put down. A vet tech there fell in love with Lucy and asked the owners if she could try to find her a home. Jan picked up on the story via Facebook and it was a done deal. Lucy is just fine with two insulin shots a day.

Steve and Jan have talked in recent years about setting up an old dog sanctuary, but that one will be a tall order. Maybe someday?

Jan tells me that there is a rescue network across Nebraska, Omaha to Sydney, mostly along the interstate. Each rescuer branches out. She has a local dog network to tie into the next area network. They try to find dogs, and it's not unusual to see Jan out looking for lost dogs. Jan has had her hands in finding, transporting, helping rehome, or paying medical bills for dozens of dogs in recent years. Steve says she must have been a detective in an earlier life because it is uncanny how she pieces things together via Facebook to solve a dog dilemma!

They help lost people, too. It's a wonder they keep it all together.

One of the things on Steve's bucket list that he developed after a few years of sobriety was setting up a halfway house. He had become acquainted with Horizon Counseling, a non-profit recovery organization in Hastings, Nebraska that runs sober living facilities for both men and women. Steve took a friend of his to a Valley Hope facility and when he was ready to leave, Steve transported him a to a Horizon sober living house. He got to know the Horizon folks and became a financial supporter of the organization.

The hope to set up a halfway house was alive and well, but Steve's workload at AgWest wouldn't allow him the time to make it happen. Jan wanted to help Steve fulfill his dream so they decided to set up a women's house with Jan acting as house manager from a distance until one of the house members could step into that role. They approached Horizon in Hastings and offered them a house in Holdrege to run under the Horizon flag and protocols. Remember that Jan had a history of an addicted boyfriend and she had completed a lot of self-help getting over those years via the Codependents Anonymous program. Jan understood program principles and was well-equipped to guide these women in their recovery.

What they were not anticipating is never, in the two years of running the house, getting to the point that one of the women in the house could assume the house-manager role. The entire time the house was open, Jan supervised and was on call basically twenty-four hours a day trying to guide some exceptionally broken women to recovery—many of which were in the house because of problems with the law and not necessarily wanting recovery.

These were battered women, addicts, and victims of sexual abuse who didn't know how to set up a checking account or do laundry. Add the lies and manipulation that often go along with this community. "Jan has a good bullshit meter, so she was the best person to spot it," Steve said.

Jan recalls: "Some of this was intuition, since I'm not an addict." This is where Steve came in. "He understood the addiction stuff and would take them to meetings in the area. I dealt with the life side of things, men and setting boundaries."

Horizon was having trouble filling the house and partway into the project they started sending girls directly out of prisons or jails. These women were there as the next step in their process of satisfying the law. It was something they had to do and not necessarily wanting to find recovery.

Jan adds: "I'm a fully capable woman, but I was out of my element. I didn't know how this worked with the parole officer. Nobody told me. I couldn't ask the parolee because they would lie to me. The second woman that moved in was a total sociopath. I knew when I met her, the bells and whistles were just going off. I don't think she was an addict. Her husband was cooking meth. Getting clean was part of her parole. At one point, we had six in the house. We had meth cookers. One gal had been in prison for home invasions. We had a total of fifteen come through the house. Every one of them had been sexually abused as a child. Some were raped or brutalized in adulthood. So, we were going to try to get them off drugs but not address this extreme trauma?

"I didn't feel like I was in danger, but my mom worried about me. I'm not big in physical stature, but I'm big otherwise! In our weekly meeting, this woman in her forties shouted about one of the rules I described: You had to earn the right to visit your family. They could come visit you at an agreed upon time, but you had to earn the right to go for an outside visit. She yelled in my face. I tend to match energy, but this time, I sat and firmly talked her down, while sitting on the edge of a rocking chair wanting to stand up and defend myself. Yet, I didn't; I knew these other young women were watching me. They didn't care what she was doing. They wanted to know how I would respond. She was like a child acting out. She sat down. I was so glad because it would have escalated.

"Some of these women were very attractive. There are people who go to recovery meetings to be predatory, sensing the weaknesses of addicts. One man we knew, who was extremely handsome, had slept with half of these girls while in the house. By the way, that was strictly against house rules. I had to talk with him about my suspicion that he was using the house as a candy store.

"When things got tough with one woman, I had to firmly remind her that I was standing between her and going back to prison, I never wanted that kind of responsibility but that's how it turned out. In a weird way, it was one of the most honest moments I've had with a human being. We both knew what I meant—if she didn't follow the house rules, I just had to call her parole officer.

"It took a long time for the women to figure out where I lived even though the house was just a few blocks away. One of them showed up at my door, and I called a meeting the next day, declaring, 'Don't ever show up at my door. If you do, there better be someone chasing you with a knife.'"

This story reminded me that addicts feel entitled sometimes. It's an extremely slanted frame of having no boundaries, too.

"An eighteen-year-old wasn't doing well. Three months into the rehab house, she started spreading a rumor that I was using her like 'slave labor'. The only task she had was mowing the lawn! [The world of addiction can get rather bizarre.] This whole endeavor helped me to define my boundaries, limits and triggers. It was quite a learning experience. I firmly believe that even the worst experience usually happens for a learning experience. My first husband was abusive, so I learned to stand up for myself.

"At the end, two of the girls went out and used all weekend. The other girl in the house invited a guy over who brought meth with him. I went to the house with Steve because someone informed us that the blinds were torn off the windows. We peered in and didn't see anyone. I was a hound dog in my former life or something. I had this urge to search the house. We found rocks of meth sitting on a stand. We confronted everyone a couple of days later. No one would admit to having the meth. I love a good detective story! I demanded that everyone empty out their packs of cigarettes on the table. I found the match of butts that were with the meth rocks. I showed her the picture of the meth and cigarette butt. By the time that conversation was over, everyone was packed up and gone. We threw all of them out, closed the door and checked the half-way house off of Steve's bucket list."

In essence, this big endeavor had been a case of giving back and going crazy because of it.

Steve and Jan didn't realize that this endeavor to help people would eventually throw Jan into the darkest time of her life. She's had terrible anxiety since. This triggered past history of PTSD. They blamed it on the house, but the house was not the core—that atmosphere brought out fight or flight in her. Since, they've been more hands-off but just as influential. They have helped with the cost of rehabs for some, including a woman with zero resources. They paid for her entire thirty-day treatment. Jan recently helped a woman find her path out of a multi-year abusive marriage. The help ranged from hours of coaching over the phone, paying her attorney's retainer fee to start the process, and providing her and her son a place to stay for three weeks while the dust settled.

This is who they are as a couple—cognizant about animals and people in need and willing to help whenever possible.

CHAPTER 18

HAUNTING HOLDREGE

Every town is unique. Every story is unique.

But you don't normally find a Halloween haunted house in the center of the action. What unites setting and plot here is busy air, addiction, altruism, and fun. Jan's attitude is: "I don't know how many years of life I have left, but I'm going to get weird with it!"

Steve and Jan have a house on a prominent street. They're on display. Jan grew up as a snot-nosed kid three blocks "that way." Her family didn't have much money. In ways, Steve and Jan are unlikely partners. For a while, she struggled with being a corporate wife and being herself. Those two don't go together. In an attempt, she went out and bought "Nancy Reagan clothes." They are no longer in her closet. She donated them.

"I was trying to make myself be what I thought I was supposed to be," she said. "I couldn't breathe. I talked to Steve and apologized for not being 'that person.'"

He exclaimed, "I never wanted you to be!"

"So, you don't care if I wear fringe to your office parties?" He said no. And so, every outfit Jan has worn to his office functions since has fringe. "I have to be me. I think I'm too damned old to be someone else. He doesn't have a cookie cutter wife."

Just what kind of wife does Steve have?

She operates a Halloween haunted house, tends to flowerbeds and animals, and is creative 24/7. During January and February, she goes into a funk because there isn't much to do with haunting or gardening in the cold months. "I'm so geared toward being creative, if it doesn't come out of me, it turns rotten," she said flatly.

Jan and her sister started out front of the house dressed as witches with a cauldron. Within two years, she recruited thirty people to dress up in their yard and Steve built walkways to keep people confined in this Halloween madness that his wife created. The last year she did a 'home haunt', they hosted a freebie of candy all night and had about 500 people visit. (Steve can still see the paths in the grass, which bugs him.)

Loving the Halloween haunt business, Jan finally found and bought a house. That house had been abandoned for two years and was filled with the objects of a hoarder, including animals. She hired a crew to clear it out and get it into the shape in order to walk through without fear of death.

Now, the haunt world is big with surprisingly large conventions. One of the main haunt sites, The Scare Factor, initiates a public vote each year on the best haunts in each state. Two years ago, Jan's landed fourth in Nebraska. Then, in 2018, Grey House Haunts moved to second place. In 2019, Jan's new and frightening antics paid off and she hit the top "must see" haunt in Nebraska. There is another site that gauges haunts and she landed second in the state in that one. It is especially a big deal when considering there are very large haunts in the Lincoln and Omaha area that would be on these lists as well.

All the publicity helped marketing for sure and Jan was incredibly proud of her invention, Grey House Haunts.

This is the kind of wife Steve has, and he couldn't be happier.

CHAPTER 19

FAMILY AND FORBIDDEN FEELINGS

Alcohol and blood are a terrifying mix. Every time. All the time.

It's widely known that people who drink can blow through the family budget, cause fights, ignore children, and otherwise impair the health and happiness of the people they love. Of married couples who get into physical altercations, 60 to 70 percent abuse alcohol. In time, family members may develop symptoms of codependency, inadvertently keeping the addiction alive, even though it harms them.

Children and extended family members, as mentioned, can become codependent on a loved one's alcohol abuse, or at least be significantly affected. According to the American Academy of Child and Adolescent Psychiatry (AACAP), 1 in every 5 adult Americans resided with a relative who abused alcohol in their adolescence. As a general rule, these people have a greater likelihood of having emotional troubles compared to children who grew up in sober homes. Early exposure to an alcoholic abuser can also increase the child's propensity to have a problematic relationship with alcohol. In general, children of individuals who abuse alcohol are four times more likely to abuse alcohol themselves. As the AACAP explains, children are in a unique position in relation to a parent or caregiver who abuses alcohol. The drinking is most often a source of confusion, and the child is unlikely to have the parent's support because the parent's behavior is the heart of the problem (however unintentionally). Children will notice radical changes in behavior, such as parent turning from happy to angry, and may falsely believe that they are the cause of these mood swings. Self-blame, guilt, frustration, and anger can emerge as the child tries to understand why the parent acts this way.

This is only the beginning.

Steve's children, Ronda, Dawn, and Jamie are all upstanding individuals. Their own stories are so illuminating. Who their father was when they were children and who he is at present paints a telling family photo that forgiveness and healing are *always* possible. But it comes with great effort; it comes with facing feelings (something Steve was not used to until recent daily work).

Being an adult child of an alcoholic myself, I know their stories matter because there are so many grim directions they could have gone in and stayed there. It's important to see the fusion of their pain and growth. In fact, Steve also realized this and wanted to keep the integrity of their perspectives by including them here in their own words.

Ronda

"I'm a registered nurse. When I was growing up, I remember it seemed like my dad always had a drink in his hand. I know he wanted to get sober, but he continued to struggle even after his first stint through rehab. I was working on a master's degree and happened to be at Mayo Clinic in Rochester doing a research symposium when Dad was at his last rehab. He was about an hour from Rochester, so I slipped out there one evening for a visit. I could see his effort, but his heart was not in it. I remember him telling me that until you hit rock bottom, it doesn't really sink in that things need to change and that you have to be the one to precipitate it. That really rang true for me, especially many years later when I myself struggled with sobriety issues.

"My first marriage ended in divorce after twenty-three years due largely in part to poor decisions fueled by alcohol abuse by both myself and my husband. I then went through a series of unhealthy relationships as I continued to drink, all of which ended badly, violently, or tragically. I ended up living with Dad and Jan a couple of times between relationships. The really sad part was, I drug both of my children through the mess. After my second marriage failed, I hit rock bottom and stopped drinking. I passed three years of sobriety in February. I had taken the same path as my dad did. He could function at work, and that is what I was doing. As soon as I got home, I needed a drink. On the way home, I would stop by the liquor store. I had the owner special-order a certain type of wine coolers and make sure there was always stock. Imagine the amount of time I was spending on alcohol, even when I wasn't drinking it. That is the root of addiction—it is the primary focus your mind makes room for.

"I never drank on the job or worked impaired. The fear of losing my nursing license was stronger than my desire to drink. That kept me sober for part of the time I needed to be sober. After work when I got home, I sat on my porch with cigarettes and booze. After I stopped drinking (and smoking!) my life took a completely different turn for the better. I rededicated my life to God, my first husband and I reconciled, and we remarried. Everything that alcohol destroyed for me is being restored.

"I work for the state. It's hard work, but it is my calling and I love what I do. I'm on the road a lot. We have an 11-year-old and a 24-year-old. My husband is sober now, too. We put our kids through the stuff I went through; however, I have a very close relationship with both of them now. They have witnessed firsthand how faith in God can rebuild lives and restore families. At 24, Kiley [Steve's meeting buddy!] just purchased her first home and has a job she loves, which allows her to dedicate time to her music. I am closer to my kids than my parents were with us. My daughter was just on vacation and didn't want to be in the atmosphere of the bars and heavy drinking. She doesn't want that lifestyle, so I am thrilled! When she was in college, she went to

Denver for a Christian mission trip and ministered to the homeless over New Year's Eve. This is where she spent her New Year's Eve when she was 19 years old. I know I wouldn't be where I'm at if God had not pulled me out of the pit I was in. Faith is what has kept me sober and I think that is why my dad has been able to maintain his sobriety. Faith is paramount."

Dawn

"To this day, I will go by a truck stop, smell diesel fumes and think about my dad taking me with him in the truck. I wasn't in school yet, so I don't know how many states we were in, but he took me all the time. My dad also took us trick or treating. I have many fond childhood memories of my dad.

"Right after they got divorced, it was difficult for us as kids to live with the hurt and anger that was between our parents. At the time, we couldn't understand why they would say and do such hurtful things to each other; often, we wondered if we were to blame. I carried an enormous amount of anxiety and guilt because I felt as though he didn't love us or want us anymore.

"Right after the divorce, money was tight. I had to get a job and worked all through high school. We struggled financially and emotionally. When Steve was in the picture, we had nice cars, clothes, house, Christmases. When the divorce happened, all that went away.

"He's been able to do something that most people are not able to do. That is, take a really good look in the mirror at who you are, where you are in life and how you influence or affect people. It is a very humbling and hard thing to do. I don't know many people who have done this successfully. When I think of Steve, I remember when he quit drinking a few weeks before my wedding. I didn't have a very good relationship with him, and we barely spoke. I was on edge about whether he would be sober at my wedding. He came and it went fine. That following Christmas, I remember thinking clearly, *I don't think I have ever met this man.* Who is this person? He cracked a joke. *Who is this guy?* It was a profound epiphany that I didn't really know him. After that time in our life, he inspired me to do great things in my own life. If he could do what he has done, I could quit smoking, quit chewing my nails, go on a diet, and be a better person. I could look in the mirror. Many times, I have thought of the magnitude of what he has done to turn his life around. Knowing somebody could do that has helped me to do that in my own life. If he had not changed, he would not be alive.

"You can't be a successful person without providing something of value to people. I'm not surprised of his success at all. It's easy to believe he has your best interest at heart, and that is why people trust him so much.

"I'm a corporate director of HR. We operate in fourteen states and have a great team. All three of us kids graduated from college, which is amazing given our upbringing. My bachelor's degree is in chemistry and mathematics. Then I was in a PhD program for a while but shifted to the real world of working before finishing. I have always been a driven person. My mother didn't graduate from high school, yet she pushed us hard. I've been in HR for twenty years.

"A lot of people are not exposed to a side of life in which they've ever had to endure, truly endure. Car not starting, basement flooding...things happen. But I'm talking about circumstances that you can't do anything about, you're not in control, so the only thing you can do is endure it. It tests who you are as a person. I don't think people realize what Steve Knuth has had to endure. He truly has steel inside of him by his own making."

Jamie

"Back then, Dad was always working and drinking a lot. He and his brothers worked 100+ hours a week during the busy seasons. When Dad started managing his own plant, he had a business landline installed at the house to make sure he'd be available at any time. The damned thing would ring day and night. The business came first. And if not working, he'd often be off somewhere else, probably the bar. These factors, combined with my mother's hot temper, didn't make for a happy marriage.

"Dad was not the model Knuth, or at least it didn't seem so back then. And over time, it felt like he was the black sheep, the wild one, the drunk of the family. Out of the five of the brothers and sisters, it always felt like he was the least put together. That shaped us as a family. At get-togethers it often made us feel like we were the black sheep, too. It took a toll on my sisters. I didn't realize it then, but looking back, I think I was closer to the Knuth family than they were. I was often at grandma's house and I'd spend summers with Dad's sister, Marilyn.

"After the divorce, Mom instilled in us that Steve was no good, a bad influence, and just a bad person. I think I reminded her of dad in many ways and that may be why her and I never saw eye to eye. She was hard on us kids, though I can honestly say she did her best to always make sure that we were taken care of, despite the hand she was dealt and her own very rocky past.

"In my early teens I moved in with Dad, which to this day, has never sat well with my mother. I wasn't fitting in well with the Holdrege school system and I wanted to go back to the farm where we lived before. Shortly after I made the move, we did just that. Dad was in his second wave of sobriety; I think he'd been sober for eight months or so. But not long after I moved in, his drinking resumed. It didn't take long for the booze to really take control. Dad once told me, 'An addiction doesn't sleep; it just waits for you.' Once you go back, it just picks up right where you left it, and in most cases, intensifies from there. In my mid-teens, I'd be calling the bars at night to see if I could find him and if so, pled with him to come home. After a while, I think he just started to tell the bartender to insist to me that he was not there. Those were some long and often confusing nights.

"By then, I had started working for the fertilizer company that Uncle Dewey owned. Dad helped him build that business up, and over time, many of the family members joined in. I started working there at an early age. For the first few summers I lived and worked with my cousin, Brad, and then with my Uncle Dewey. Brad taught me a lot but working for Dewey was quite an experience. In family settings he was an honest and forthright Christian that was always very supportive and understanding. At work, however, he had an exceptionally high expectancy of people and what their capabilities should be. He expected excellence and very hard work. He could bring me to tears for disappointing him, and for a while I wanted to change my family name.

"Though he was reluctant, Dad gave me the opportunity to do those things. He never said it was going to be easy. I was a kid doing responsible work, learning how to operate highly technical machines, being trained and certified to perform very specific labor-intensive duties. I was crushing 100-hour weeks alongside people twice my age. It was such a brutal and turbulent time, but in many ways, it has helped mold who I am today. Having lived through that, I can honestly say it was one of the most valuable and rewarding experiences of my life.

"I followed right into my dad's footsteps in a lot of ways. I had my wild streaks and crazy nights, long hauls and my fair share of mistakes. I've had my own run-ins with drugs and alcohol, turbulent relationships, and moments of deep despair. But throughout all of it, Dad was always there. Whether he was up or down, put together or not, he never once gave up on me. And he was always willing to give words of advice and support.

"I'm a father now, and like most parents I see the world very differently. I have a lot of respect and compassion for both of my parents and what they went through. They were both trying to do the best they could. Dad had so many fronts to deal with; he tried to kick alcohol more than a few times, helped build and run a demanding business, took on two adopted kids and a hot-tempered wife with a son on the way, working side-by-side with his brothers who worked nonstop. We were all influenced through his experiences, and there were many.

"But see, Steve's a man of many colors and he has had many phases in his life. He's been untogether and put back together, the dependent and the rock. He's solidly confident but has also been very insecure about many things. He's a man of conviction and perseverance, compassion and understanding. Many of the struggles have been put there by him or by others. He's my dad, my best friend and my confidant. He's one of the strongest people I've ever known.

"We've all learned from his successes and his failures. And in the latter, he's a very self-reflecting person. Maybe too much sometimes. He really beats himself up about a lot of things. Even things that are out of his control. In doing that, he has learned a lot about himself and about others. He can relate to so many different types of people and their experiences. He's fallen and put himself back together numerous times. It's through those fallen times and reflections of his own mistakes that has made him change himself time and time again. I say that because he focuses on those times more than his successes. That's quite a statement considering that he's an extremely successful person as a human being. He's been able to channel his own journey to help people as he recognizes their struggles. His past is not a closed chapter, but rather one that defines him.

"In every way, he's a man of his word. And if he says he's there for you, he will be. No matter if it's in the dead of winter or the dead of night, he'll do what he can to help and support anyone. He'll give anyone a chance, and lord knows he's given me thousands! He's not perfect, and he doesn't expect perfection from other people. He makes mistakes, like we all do. But the mistakes he's made and even the ones to come, they are lessons to learn from, even if sometimes they are those of regret.

"He's often apologized to me and my sisters about our upbringing. He's gone to great lengths to right the wrongs he's done unto others. And he's even called himself a bad dad a time or two. What he probably doesn't realize is that for me, he's the best dad I could have ever asked for, and I am eternally blessed to be a part of his life."

If you have issues or unresolved pieces from your family of origin, they will come out in your relationships. Steve has done many hours looking at family dynamics and life history, patterns that tend to repeat and why they are repeating, and his own personal inner psychology of why he thinks the way he does and where his behaviors come from, along with whom he is trying to become.

Psychologist Chuck Rhodes advocates that this is "basic" psychological work that everyone needs to do to become healthy. It doesn't matter whether or not you were raised in a really healthy environment or a very dysfunctional one, we all have basic issues we need to address at some point. Small traumas or issues that we didn't navigate well in key developmental periods, so we get stuck. It helps to have a third party help us go back and retrace it, clean it up, and help us move forward.

Chuck has a varied background. He was seminary-trained with a master's divinity degree, worked in a local church for a few years, went back for a doctorate in clinical psychology, and then opened up a clinical practice. Fast-forward twenty years later, after obtaining other degrees in organizational psychology, he's been able to blend the field of clinical psychology, with leadership development and work training and development. The two of them fit nicely together and translate over to the business world. Thus, his work with Steve!

Steve was a reluctant participant at first, but in order to be a better father, husband and leader, he knew he had to get a handle on his family and not just his kids, whose stories all end in forgiveness and healing thankfully.

Steve and Chuck met through Valley Hope, where Chuck's practice was a partnering consultant in the search for a CEO during the nine-month interim. Impressed, Steve was encouraged to hire him for leadership development at AgWest and personal development for Steve. Both were intertwined. Chuck's findings were sometimes uncanny but always intriguing and helpful.

According to Chuck, Steve's basic family was extremely dysfunctional, one of the most dysfunctional systems he has encountered in all his years of practice. Steve and his sister, Marilyn, participated in a four-hour session around "family of origin," and it was a much deeper dive into family than what Steve did in all three treatment centers.

Chuck broke the Knuth family down. Each one of the five kids came out their upbringing with their own coping mechanism. Three of four hours into the session with Steve and Marilyn, he said, "I'm amazed you all turned out as well as you did." Professional successes.

Chuck's assessment is a profound book about Steve in itself. I place the lengthier description because it details the family as a system—one that we all possess. When addiction operates the system, you see the different phases of dysfunction and how it crosses generations.

"You have intergenerational dysfunction that starts with the grandparents, which is the furthest back we traced because this is the info we had. Typically, patterns cut across generations for as long as you can trace the family tree. What you had is a series of parents and adults who were in charge of raising children within systems and the parents were psychologically unhealthy themselves so they lacked the inner resources necessary to be able to provide children the care and attention and structure and boundaries, everything that goes along with raising healthy children. These parents were unable to provide this, so the children were raised in an emotionally deprived environment where it was every man or woman for himself or herself. In psychological care that a child needs, the attention they need to emotionally unfold in a healthy way and accept themselves for the good and bad, strengths and weaknesses—that type of guidance was not provided because the parents never received it themselves. They were so emotionally involved or caught up in their own life drama and concerns, they didn't have the resources to care for the children in a way that would stimulate healthy development and growth. If the parents are not healthy, more than likely they're highly self-involved and egocentric. Their primary concern is meeting their own inner deficiencies and unmet needs. They will typically do this through their children so the children themselves become vehicles for parents to get their needs met.

"In this system, there was a lot of emotional neglect, emotional abuse, anger was used as a weapon to control and manipulate, so kids raised in this system do one of two things: Act out and rebel or become complacent and dependent. Almost all of them exhibited strong signs of dependent personality disorder. The heart and soul of dependent personality disorder is you become who you think others want you to become rather than who you really are as a person, so you can get the approval you crave. All the kids in the system craved the approval of their parents—the problem was there wasn't any to go around! Whatever love or attention, all the kids fought over it. Each developed their own adaptive mechanisms to be able to get the attention, care they craved:

- The oldest brother became a superstar in the business world. He over-functioned and became a workaholic.

- The oldest daughter acquired some of the characteristics of the father and grandmother. She became the matriarch of her family and could at times be controlling and critical. Unlike the father and grandmother, she also had a big heart and loved her family more than anything.

- Third in line, the middle child was the sibling that has always been closest to Steve. Marilyn became a caregiver, a good girl who needed purpose. As an adult, she found a wonderful man/husband who became a minister. She has often told Steve that she could have followed his path into the darker side if it were not for her husband, Bob.

- The youngest brother became a tough guy, went into the military directly from high school.

- Steve's strategy was to become a nice guy. The archetypal nice guy syndrome: They give up their own wants and needs in order to be able to satisfy people so they will be liked, avoid confrontation, internalize anger and pretend nothing is wrong, so they won't upset other people. Steve has spent his adult life being the preverbal nice guy who won't push back, so people have taken advantage of him. This plays out in the business world, too.

"Steve has had to deal with being able to express anger, set boundaries, say no, push back on people he cares about. If he doesn't care about someone, he doesn't have a problem telling you to fuck off, which is what a healthy person would do. But if he cares about you and what you think about him, he flips into nice guy mode and is literally emotionally incapable of setting boundaries, having difficult conversations, and processing anger. There is a whole range. Now, these dependency patterns play out in your professional leadership. He has been an ineffective leader when it comes to making good business decisions around personal and emotional issues because of the pattern.

"As a child, it was not acceptable for him to be angry because there was already anger in the system. He learned that the best way to manage was to swallow it and not process any of the emotions that come in any human's life. He became frightened of his own anger. What about addiction? His journey as a leader? When you spend your life swallowing your anger, it's common to develop a disorder, dysthymic disorder. Low-grade depression that is not bio-chemical. It's individuals who have been swallowing anger for an extended period of time. Anger turned inward becomes some form of depression. The heart and soul of depression is a series of feeling helpless, hopeless, hapless. Severe depression often forms as lack of self-acceptance, of self-hatred. They can carry this low-grade depression their whole lives. You have this and a significant stressor, like Susan's death, it can turn into full-blown depression for a long period of time. Right now, we're trying to help him develop healthy techniques to accept and process anger. But alcohol for twenty-seven years equaled more than a third of his life drinking. Alcohol here is self-medication, an attempt to deal with inner emotions that he never dealt with—family of origin stuff, relationships and mistakes.

"Late teens to 40s, he was in a self-destructive cycle. The message you internalize from parents is, *I'm not worthy.* If this message forms your self-identity, you try to create what should be inside from the external world. The inside is a mess. Then we try to find a sense of congruity between inner and outer. If someone has a high level of condemnation, there is a lot of judgment toward oneself, and then they create an external world that mirrors the internal, so it is reinforcing. Self-destructive behavior is about self-hatred. It's not self-conscious. We act as if the "world is against us and we have bad luck." No, you're making bad choices! We make choices that mirror how we feel about ourselves. In professional coaching, you go in and try to deconstruct that early self and begin to replace it with a healthier version of your inner sense of self. Only then will the outer world begin to change. You can be a person with flaws and a lot of good qualities. When we synthesize the good and bad into a coherent, healthy system, we begin to create a world that is different and healthier.

"KEY: Anytime the inner and the outer are not congruent, then we feel anxiety. If I feel self-hatred and if things are going really well, that does not feel right. We call it being 'ego-dystonic.' So, in order to alleviate that anxiety, we create an external environment that is negative and destructive, and based on failure. When things are going well even, in the back of their mind, there is this feeling like, when are things going to go bad? They will unconsciously make decisions to make sure that happens. Even though it feels bad, at least it is congruent."

Thinking of others in my own life who had exhibited exactly what Chuck described, I found this absolutely profound: If a self-sabotaging person doesn't make that bad outer world, the anxiety is more of the problem than the actual problem, which is what is unresolved *inside*.

The anxiety is crippling. They need to remove the anxiety. That is the thought process, without even knowing it. This also leads to sabotage of something going really well. The original wound is the childhood wound, internalized messages from your mom or dad about whether you're acceptable, loveable or what not; then the rest of our lives, we add insult to injury, wound on top of wound. If you never processed, you have layers and layers of unresolved issues, of trauma, of psychological struggles that have not been addressed. With several layers, you get a strong amount of force where it takes a lot of time, tension, and therapy to deconstruct all this.

Chuck adds: "The idea of an archaeologist is a good metaphor. You're going layer by layer of dysfunction, trying to clean it up and translating it in such a way that is healthier. If we don't translate correctly, it gets mistranslated and this can go on forever. The trick is going down far enough to where you can create a semblance of health and energy to continue on until out of this cycle."

Being able to internalize all of this and swallow the meaning is, indeed, proof that Steve is more than keen to break the cycle.

CHAPTER 20

THE TERMINAL UNIQUENESS CLUB

What is Steve's relationship with alcohol now?

He had tried so hard to quit for so long without success. Once making it, he was scared to death to go in a bar. He wouldn't even walk up the booze aisle in a Walmart. He was afraid of catching sight of a CC bottle and it becoming an unmanageable trigger.

Another association to kick is that he loved to go to Las Vegas and gamble. He's only been there once since sobering up. He looks at the process of being sober like the grieving process. There are different stages and it never fully goes away.

His company holds multiple meetings each year where they offer an open bar. Steve jokes that as much as he drank for twenty-seven years, he is sure he has bought more booze since being sober than before. His wife, Jan, drinks a beer or half-beer occasionally and she usually has part of a six-pack in their kitchen fridge. That doesn't bother him but still today, he does not want a CC bottle in the house. He doesn't tolerate being in a setting late night when people are getting drunk and not simply enjoying a drink over dinner or in a social setting. He feels it has more to do with a reminder of what he was, no doubt, like, rather than a desire to be along with them for the ride.

No longer a drinker, Steve is quite a thinker! But he admits to having one bad habit left.

You had a little preview, but he loves the game of blackjack. Actually, he loves the thrill of the gamble. Chuck provided a scientific explanation to what it does to Steve's brain: Forget about everything else while in the zone and a great run at a "BJ" table is pretty exhilarating! Check out the following Kolbe assessment of Steve.

All falls under a risk-taking mentality: Drink hard for twenty-seven years. Smoke way too much for forty-seven years. Live on the edge with questionable lifestyle for much of the drinking years.

One of his problems in getting sober was the "terminal uniqueness" mindset. As a reminder, his counselor, Carol, got irritated with Steve at some point and told him that to get something out of rehab, all he had to do was spend half his time looking for similarities to other patients rather than spending all his time finding reasons that he wasn't like them. She urged Steve that if he didn't, he would die of *terminal uniqueness*.

Steve knew he wasn't stupid and therefore, "should" have been able figure out why he drank the way he did and ultimately, fix it. The first problem with this is there are too many "I's" in that statement and in that entire thought. It all boiled down to acceptance or inability to accept that he was an alcoholic and needed to deal with things as such.

Step #1 of the 12 steps: "We admitted we were powerless over alcohol—that our lives had become unmanageable."

If a person cannot embrace step 1, the rest of the steps are useless. Steve knew deep in his heart that there was something wrong with him that made him drink. He wanted to find and fix that, so basically, he could just drink more reasonably, right? He didn't realize until he was sober for a couple of years that he was absolutely right about one thing. There were and are things wrong with his internal makeup that likely weighed into his becoming an alcoholic. What Steve missed all those years was one simple fact: He could not begin to address the core issues unless the alcohol was removed completely. *Acceptance* was a big stumbling block for

Steve Knuth and I suspect for most everyone who cannot achieve sobriety.

Chuck went on to pinpoint why Steve enjoys gambling so much. It does something to the same part of the brain as chemical addiction. Read Steve's own romantic description of gambling and tell me it doesn't read like a boy's experiences in a candy store:

"My first gambling experience happened when I was 19 or 20 years old. In my small town of Oxford, there was a monthly gun club stag, with food, booze and a craps game. I think it was the first time I went to one of these events and there was certainly plenty of drinking going on. The craps game looked intriguing and after some explanation, I joined in. I have no idea how or what exactly happened but suddenly, I was the big winner! A guy who I didn't know from a different town ran out of cash and wanted to keep playing with IOUs. I was all right with that and pretty soon, had him owning me $800. This was my first and significant lesson about gambling. I make the following statement to folks often while sitting at table in casinos: 'It's not hard to make money in a casino but it's darned hard to get out the door with any of it.' That night, my first introduction to the thrill of gambling, I had the guy owning me $800 and before we quit, I owed him $1,100 that I didn't have.

"Before I go on to talk about a lifetime of gambling, there is more to the story above. I got $500 of the $1,100 to the guy fairly soon but back in the early 70s, that was a pile of money. I didn't get any more to him and he called me one Sunday afternoon a few years later, wondering if I could even up. I was married by then and had taken on a ready-made family with two little girls. I didn't have his money and in fact, we were really struggling to stay above water. I told him as much and to his credit, he never contacted me again. That was back in the mid-70s, which is important to the rest of this story.

"When I finally sobered up in 1998 after ten years of treatment centers and relapses, it was time to do things differently, time to make some amends. A year or so into sobriety, I realized that if had a quarter for every time I thought about the $600 I owed the guy, it would have been paid off several times over. In other words, it had bugged me for twenty-five years or so. I wrote the guy a short note explaining that I was at a point in life where I needed to clean up the past rubble. I didn't explain alcoholism or what I had gone through to get to this point. I simply apologized for never getting it taken care of and told him I had done some simple compounding interest since the mid-70s and came up with something over $2,000 that I owned him. I think that I sent a note and a check for $2,500!

"Understand that I did that more for me than him. That's what Step #9 is about—making amends. It's what one needs to try to do to put the past behind and move forward. Of interest though, Gene, the guy I lost money to, was a farmer from forty miles away from my hometown. Within the first year of starting AgWest, he walked into my office. It was a bit uncomfortable when I realized who he was (hadn't seen him since that night in the 70s), but he smoothed it over very nicely. He said he appreciated the check and note and that he, too, had hit a point in his life where he had to clean up some things. He never mentioned alcohol and I had not mentioned it in my note to him, but it was like we both understood. After a short acknowledgement about that, he said he wanted to set up a trading account.

"Gambling as an addiction? I was hooked from the beginning. Back in the late 70s and throughout the 80s, there were no casinos outside of Las Vegas or Atlantic City. In this part of the world, direct flights were pretty reasonable to Las Vegas. I didn't have any money to blow but when you have an addiction, you figure things out. The early years of going to Vegas I remember taking $300 for gambling. Somehow on small stakes tables, I generally made that work for the two or three days there.

"I don't remember how many times I went to Vegas before local casinos came into being but would guess I made it two or three times a year with some regularity. I had some decent wins at times back then, which only strengthens the addiction. I remember my first big win. It was back in the 1980s at the Lady Luck in Las Vegas. I was on a table that became a dumping table where everyone was winning. Very unusual and I've never seen anything quite like what happened that evening since. The dealer started breaking a lot and it happened for quite some time. There was one guy from Texas at our table who was gambling pretty big even before the table turned good. I would guess he walked away from that table $15,000 to $20,000 ahead. I was gambling my small chunks but as I got ahead, I upped the stakes. Remember that I was up to $200 bets, which was heart stopping for me at that time. I left that table up $5,000 and before I knew it, I had a casino host moving me from my cheap room to a comped suite on the top floor. I tried to sleep but couldn't. I got up and went back to gambling because man, I wanted more of that feeling. Before I left Vegas, I had lost it all.

"I've always gambled a little more than I should for my financial status, but I've never taken it to the point of taking food off the table or causing inability to pay the bills. Notice what I just did; that is no more than a statement of justification. Us addicted folks (no matter to what) are great at justification—we have it down to an art form!

"Anyway, as success happened with AgWest and my financial condition improved, the stakes rose over the years. I've often joked that it ain't gambling unless it can hurt. There is a whole lot of truth to that statement. I came up with that many years back and it has proven to be true throughout my life. If today, I took $300 into a casino and walked out with nothing, it would not move the excitement needle. Truth is, I wouldn't even consider gambling at those stakes today because it would not provide me what I need out of the risk/reward ratio. It would be incredibly boring.

"In current times, I try to limit risk to $5,000 on a given trip to a casino, but I sometimes lose my discipline and it goes above that amount. I think the worst one-time loss ever in a single trip into a casino was around $15,000. I beat myself up over that quite a little bit. Losing discipline is a problem in many aspects of life and gambling is no different. On the winning side of things and the reason one keeps going back, I have had some thrills.

"This certainly doesn't happen often but the cards (I play blackjack mostly) ebb and flow. When the cards shift in your favor, one needs to start pressing the bets. As my financial ability has improved, I have become very aggressive at pressing to larger bets. That can get pretty costly when what appears to be a run in the making falls apart. But occasionally, the stars seem to align, and you end up winning hand after hand, losing very few in a string of twenty or twenty-five hands. That's when the aggressive gambler will have a blast. Those runs never last long in terms of time. Generally, a great run will unfold and be done within twenty minutes or less. But a lot of great action can happen in that short spell.

"Some notable winnings. A few years back at the Ameristar in Council Bluffs, Iowa, I was the only person at a table with a six-deck shoe. It was a normal

$10 table where anyone could have joined at any time, but amazingly, no one else set down during that run. During that one six-deck shoe, I won over $8,000. That happened in ten to fifteen minutes. Also, at the Ameristar, I sat down at a $25 table and only had thirty minutes or so before I had to meet someone for dinner. After a few minutes of give and take, I hit a run that garnered over $11,000 before dinner.

"My largest win ever happened recently at a casino in Davenport, Iowa. I was there for three nights while doing presentations for our newest branch office. The first night, I went back to the room up $13,000, which was one of my top ten wins of all time. The next night, I went to the casino for less than three hours and cracked out the best all-time win of my life taking over $21,000 back to the room. For the first time in my life, I accepted the offer to have security walk me to my room.

"The following night, I did a presentation thirty miles north of Davenport and was carrying nearly $40,000 around in my briefcase. I always have cash with me, but that was a bit unnerving.

"Those are cool stories and gamblers love to boast about the wins. We just tend to skip any elaboration about losing our discipline or getting on a ten-casino-trip losing streak. Those things happen. They don't build those flashy buildings on losses. The odds 'are what they are' and the casinos had them figured out in their favor long before I was born. Short of cheating or card counting, folks don't win in the long run, and I'm not smart enough for either of those activities."

So, what makes an ordinary person keep going back when there is no hope of long-term success? That is the insidious part of an addiction... any addiction. When the gambling gets painful enough or Steve simply comes to grips with not needing that excitement, he suspects he can find abstinence with that addiction as well. Time will tell. In the meantime, he will likely chase that next $10,000 win!

In all this chasing and clamoring for risk and excitement, Steve struggles with depression, or at least low-grade depression. Chuck gave Steve the clinical diagnosis of living in some level of depression all the time. Steve came out of that session sad. He looked at his life as a sad mother bear. Some things can spike him out of it, but he tends to maintain this animal that never goes away. One solution is maintaining the attitude of gratitude: "If I could get up every day and live that way, depression wouldn't be that big of a deal."

Jan knows when Steve is slipping because he gets quiet and says he does not know what is wrong. That is the problem. She then helps him track the root of him feeling this way. *When did it start? Let's figure out the event, the trigger. You can't just stare at the TV and expect the answer to tumble out! You have to think about it, work on it.* Jan has done a lot of this. She had a breakdown, took medication and was in therapy for three and a half years. Most of the time, she figures it out and evolves by herself, but she needs a plan.

"Tonight, I'm upset, I need sleep and first thing tomorrow, I will do X, Y, Z," Jan insists. "Steve and people like him tend to get stuck on feeling bad and don't move through next steps. It took me a while to sympathize with him 'not knowing.' It's frustrating. I've had moments of just being in the dumps and not knowing why but eventually you make connections, make a link. For instance, my dad died during this month and I always feel bad this time of year. If you put it together and give yourself permission to feel and express, it kind of dissolves. But if you are out of touch with your feelings, you can't put it together, can you?"

Chuck affirmed that befriending anger and sadness as a part of the normal human spectrum of life is essential. It's okay to experience these emotions; they won't overwhelm or destroy you. You can welcome them, accept them and try to decode them. All emotions are nothing more than energy and motion; each one carries a different message that you need. Early warning or detection signals that something is going on inside of you or the environment that you need to pay attention to. They're like flashing lights. When an emotion comes, it's like a wave crashing on shore. If you pay attention to it, the intensity of the wave decreases. If you push it down, the intensity will grow and grow and grow. If you repress emotions, they are not serving their purpose.

At some point, these emotions will turn into symptoms. Depression is internalized anger.

Chuck added: "Now, recognize those are some depressive symptoms. Between low-grade and clinical/full-blown, there are major differences. In clinical, we need to increase the level of serotonin. The problem is there is no research that serotonin is the solution—pharma companies push drugs that do make a difference for some and for others, they do not. As Steve works his way through this fog, it may clear up and he can just enjoy life. The flip side is there is a part of him that likes to gamble. Because he has pushed his emotions down, he is 'dysthymic'—he does not feel alive. What he has to do in order to feel that he is alive is take greater and greater risks. Gambling is a mechanism by which he can feel what a normal, healthy person feels on a daily basis. People who use drugs, initially there is a powerful rush, but after you continue to use, what happens is that high is not strong. People with dysthymic disorder have lost their ability to connect to normal joy in life so they search for joy. Taking risks is enough of a challenge to feel alive for people with this disorder. If he didn't have the money he has, it could be a problem! It's pleasure seeking, chasing after a feeling that he has shut down."

Death of a true love, systems, family of origin, depression every day of your life, escaping addiction... escaping addiction! Truly so much information to take in regarding one human being. How was Steve Knuth thriving? His staff offered the following comments, which replaced any doubts on what may lie ahead for him:

Steve is the leader and the face of the company. He has not necessarily wanted to be the face of the company. He never held himself out as the trading guru or the knowledge guru. In this industry, that is the common way. In this line of work, there are a lot of narcissists and egos.

We're all a part of this company and model. He so often tells us how blessed he is to have the right people. I've always been amazed at his sense of delegation. He trusts us.

I was thinking of how different the world would be if everyone practiced this and got out of the way.

He knows when things need to get done, it will. He trusts that the best outcome will happen in others' hands.

The timing for AgWest has not been more perfect. No one else was doing risk management.

We want to get the top dollar for our customers, and it's the Hero Syndrome. I think we worry about this more than the customers.

Steve and his brothers could get people to do things, work harder and take more pride in their work than they would ever do on their own. I see it in this group and our whole company.

There are a lot of companies that respect what we do and how we do it. They want to be like us. We built this ahead of the curve.

Steve could be gone tomorrow, and nothing will change in how we operate. The model we follow means so much to him and it's embedded. He recognizes you can force people to do something, or it can be their idea, their effort. If we don't believe in what we're trying to sell to the customer, we will struggle to do it.

That comes back to laying the foundation and finding the correct people to carry on what we started. We're all proud to say where we work.

CHAPTER 21

EVERY LIFE, EVERY CHANCE

Steve went through three full-blown treatment centers over a ten-year period of time before he could wrap his mind around the program. Before he could wrap his mind around being powerless over alcohol. The idea of ever becoming grateful to be a recovering alcoholic was so foreign to Steve, it just as well had been in another world far and gone. He did not want to see himself as one of those people. He worked hard for years to find the differences between those people and him. It was all a part of the process that eventually leads the lucky ones to the point of surrender. Some, far too many, never find that surrender point—they tap out while arriving at the moment where one either gives up the fight or ends it all in the most permanent fashion.

An attitude of gratitude took a long time after the booze was gone, but for those who can post enough time, most do become amazingly grateful. Grateful to be one of the small percentages that survive. Grateful to have an opportunity to live a completely different life. Grateful for the things they have been able to learn about life because of the addiction. Grateful for the opportunities that come their way to help others suffering from addictions.

I found Steve's friend, Brennan Vaverek's description to be quite compelling as a lasting impression: "Every human being has an odd set of characteristics that make them unique in who they are. Steve's focus is on people. He attributes the success of AgWest to a lot of luck; okay, but he instills great loyalty. That has enabled him to build an incredible team. I've seen him with struggles, but his approach is to try to help fix the person, understanding not everything can be fixed. How do we work with that? It's a thought process that change is part of the organizational whole on how people interact. When there is a problematic person on a staff, no matter how good that person is, everyone else would just fire that person. Not Steve! He has an uncanny ability to focus on tomorrow. It's never too late. Steve was forty-five when he sobered up. He started a company working out of his house and he grabbed that. He didn't have to live in the shadows of anyone, including his brother who sold a very successful business. One time, I asked him how he got through Susan's death because I was struggling with a demon. I needed that kind of strength. It's just a test of perseverance. It didn't occur to me to ask Steve about his spirituality. I'm Catholic and come from a family of priests. He does not judge anyone, but Steve has a spiritual grounding that has allowed him to persevere. For those of us who are lucky enough to be his friend, what a model of friendship. Steve is the type of friend I want to be to other people. The sermon in our church the other day was "the good Samaritan." I was thinking of that person as Steve."

Chuck Rhodes took a different approach toward a broader message for all: "The first thing is to be able to articulate the courage to be able to look at your life and do this work and be self-reflective. Your willingness to confront and overcome whatever deficiency so you can continue to grow and unfold as a person. That takes a tremendous amount of courage and energy. Quite frankly, most people do not have the courage to undergo this process, embrace their flaws, and to change. It takes high levels of psychological mindedness. Most people are not this, so they don't see the engines and connections between how you were raised, patterns and how you behave today. Steve has reached a point where he is courageously looking at himself in an effort to be able to leave a legacy of hope, health and happiness."

But I have to give Steve the last word. "I smoked for forty-seven years and quit two years ago. Most people who drink too much smoke too much. With the help of a hypnotist, I quit smoking after I was diagnosed with COPD. If I live long enough, I will have to be on oxygen. Everything I did was too hard on the body. June is a big month in my life. I stopped drinking twenty-one years ago last June, started AgWest one year later in June, and I stopped smoking two years ago in June of 2017. I'm down to just one bad habit. Maybe I'll stop gambling in June, but probably not next June."

HAPPIER HOURS

My name is Steve, and I am a grateful recovering alcoholic. To be clear, I am one of millions of folks who have found their path to recovery of which each and everyone has a story worth telling. That said, there are tens of millions of folks who continue to suffer from the addiction of drugs or alcohol and if this book, if my story, will help even one person take that first step toward recovery, it will have been a worthwhile project.

Truth be told, this didn't start out as a recovery story. The original idea behind this book was a documentation of time-tested principles for successful agricultural marketing. I envisioned the majority of the message being geared toward helping producers manage the emotions that can easily derail the best of marketing plans. The backbone of the book was going to be a "Top 10" rules list for production marketing that was a collaborative effort of the AgWest team over many years. I felt confident that drilling deep into those rules and drawing obvious analogies between the struggles of production marketing and the typical difficulties of life could help folks improve on one of the most difficult projects they face each and every year...the endeavor of marking what they produce.

Partway into the process, it became apparent to the author of my story, Candi Cross, and me that there was a recovery story to be told—a far more important book than any production-marketing guide. Sharing my path to recovery has the potential of sparking the first steps to recovery of another suffering addict. Sharing my story has the potential of saving a life and changing the lives of those close to the suffering addict. The shift from marketing principles to a recovery story was an easy one when weighing the potential impact of each.

There are two people who have made this book possible. I want to acknowledge my appreciation and gratitude to my wife, Jan, who encouraged me to do something that did not come all that easy: talking about me. Without her, this project would have never gotten off the ground. I also extend a monster "THANK YOU" to Candi Cross, the author, for her patience in listening to my ramblings and for her attention to detail. Writing is not one of my strengths and without her help, this project would have never materialized. I am quite humbled and extremely grateful to Candi for selecting my story to fully explore and attach her name to. Thank you, Candi! It has been a wonderful experience working with you and an absolute pleasure getting to know you.

I also want to say thank you to the many family, friends and employees who provided Candi time and input into my story. To be honest, I found that part of the project a little unnerving. On the one hand, I hoped for folks to provide honest input from their vantage point, and on the other hand, I wasn't sure I wanted to read about myself through others' eyes. Nonetheless, thank you to each of you who played a part in the memorialization of my life.

I would be amiss if I didn't acknowledge those who were profoundly responsible for molding me into the person I have become. That list is far too long to address here. I am what I am today because of many, but there were four folks who were primarily responsible for my finding sobriety and finding an entirely different life.

Although we lived five hours apart, my sister, Marilyn, via the phone was my lifeline during some very dark times. She was literally the difference between life and death more than one time. Had it not been for her, I would have not been here to eventually find a life that didn't require my mind to be altered on a daily basis. Thank you, sis...more than you will ever know!

My councilor during both visits to Valley Hope in Norton, Kansas, was Carol Schoenthaler. She was a counselor at Valley Hope for much of her working career. I felt a close connection with Carol and very much wanted to show her I could become a better person. That didn't happen directly following either stay at Valley Hope but the Valley Hope approach to sobriety and particularly Carol's influence on me laid a solid foundation that I was able to build on after my final rehab. The fact that Carol hung onto my cup for ten years awaiting my sober return meant so very much to me. I am thrilled to be one of her MANY success stories. Thank you, Carol!

Without question, the main player in my path to sobriety was Susan Platt, who was my significant other at a critical, life-defining moment in time. I am sober today only through the Grace of God and because of a very strong-willed woman who was not afraid to lay on me a heavy dose of "tough love". The other key player in my getting my legs under this program of sobriety was Keith Poyser, my AA sponsor. He didn't start out as my sponsor because I didn't want one, but he did start calling me with regularity just to check in and see if I was coming to the next meeting. Basically, he adopted me without putting the idea of a "sponsor" in the conversation. Both Susan and Keith have departed this world, but I have no doubt that they watch over me today. I hope that I have made them proud in some ways and I am sure that at times I have made them both roll their eyes. Let me make one thing absolutely clear: I found a path to sobriety, not perfection!

I hope you enjoyed the read and found parts to be entertaining. More than anything though, I wanted the reader to gain an understanding about addiction and that it eventually becomes a battle between life and death. The ultimate goal of this book is this: I pray that one or more who are bound by the chains of addictions find encouragement from my story, take action, and begin the journey of their own recovery.

—Steve Knuth

REFERENCES

Interviews by the Author

AgWest Staff. In-person roundtable. July 23, 2019.

Dawn Dierking. In-person interview. July 24, 2019.

Jim Engler. In-person interview. July 24, 2019.

Jim Hodge. In-person interview. July 24, 2019.

Roger and Ronda Johnson. In-person interview. July 24, 2019.

Jamie Knuth. Phone interview. August 1, 2019.

Jan Knuth. In-person interview. July 22, 2019.

Ronda Knuth. Phone interview. July 17, 2019.

Paul Mussman. In-person interview. July 22, 2019.

Dolorous Poyser. In-person interview. July 23, 2019.

Chuck Rhodes. Phone interview. August 8, 2019.

Jeff Swanson. In-person interview. July 24, 2019.

Carrie Trompke. In-person interview. July 22, 2019.

Brennan Vaverek. In-person interview. July 22, 2019.

Marilyn Zieg. In-person interview. July 22, 2019. Phone interview. March 31, 2019.

Publications

AgWest Commodities

https://www.goagwest.com

Alcoholics Anonymous World Services. Big Book, Basic Text of AA (4th Edition, 2001). [Since the first edition appeared, in 1939, it has helped millions of men and women recover from alcoholism. Chapters describing the AA recovery program remain unchanged. New stories have been added to the personal histories.]

Alliance for the Future of Agriculture in Nebraska

https://becomeafan.org

Bebensee, Ashley. "South Central Area Recovery Plans Center in Holdrege." Kearney Hub. October 28, 2019.

https://www.kearneyhub.com/news/local/south-central-area-recovery-plans-center-in-holdrege/article_569a38e6-f997-11e9-83c2-8b865a01d2c6.html

Burnette, Marshall. "SILO: Edge of the Real World." https://www.marshallburnette.com/silo-edge-of-the-real-world

Valley Hope

https://valleyhope.org/about/

CANDI S. CROSS

Candi S. Cross is the founder of You Talk I Write, a modern ghostwriting agency. She has co-developed approximately 130 books with authors worldwide. Candi is committed to helping diverse individuals with contemporary stories that make a difference. She lives in New York City with her wife and 24/7 muse, Liza. For more info, visit www.youtalkiwrite.com.

STEVEN KNUTH

Steven Knuth brings four decades of agricultural experience and more than 25 years of market analysis. He has traded futures and options since 1988 and has been a licensed commodity broker since 1990. Steven was raised on a farm in South Central Nebraska and has been directly involved in various aspects of agriculture throughout his working career. Founding AgWest Commodities in 1999, Steven set out to build the premier grain marketing service in the Midwest based on integrity, professionalism and the highest level of customer service. He understands the challenges producers face and delivers a straightforward message on current markets, risk and opportunity. AgWest has grown from a one-man shop in the basement of a farmhouse to today's 50-member team in 10 offices across the Midwest.